MOROCCO

A CULINARY JOURNEY WITH RECIPES
from the SPICE-SCENTED MARKETS OF MARRAKECH
to the DATE-FILLED OASIS OF ZAGORA

text and photographs by
JEFF KOEHLER

CHRONICLE BOOKS
SAN FRANCISCO

Library of Congress Cataloging-
in-Publication Data available.

ISBN 978-0-8118-7738-1

Manufactured in China

Designed by Alice Chau
Typesetting by Helen Lee
Map illustration on page 19
by Stephanie Welter

10 9 8 7 6 5 4 3 2 1

Chronicle Books LLC
680 Second Street
San Francisco, California 94107
www.chroniclebooks.com

for Maia, Alba, and Eva

CONTENTS

INTRODUCTION

The food of Morocco is rich, sensual, and colorful, sophisticated and artfully presented. From the vast array of small plates offering fresh and cooked "salads" that begin or accompany meals to the delicate sweet-meats (and, inevitably, mint tea), this North African kitchen not only delights but surprises.

It begins with the blending of flavors. The sweet-ness of chilled cooked carrots countered with earthy cumin, fresh parsley, and intense, unfiltered olive oil. Grated raw carrots soaked in freshly squeezed orange juice with a touch of sugar and a few drops of aromatic orange flower water, served equally as a salad or as a dessert. A purée of cucumbers with orange juice, sweetened slightly with sugar but also a generous pinch of a dried wild oregano called *zaâtar*—intimating the arid countryside—is a delight-fully refreshing drink or dessert on warm afternoons. In winter, glasses of mint tea laced with fresh, silvery absinthe leaves, marjoram, or lemon verbena, even saffron threads. And the main dishes! Braised lamb topped with orange segments soaked in aromatic syrup and with thin, candied strips of peel; kid goat with dried figs and thyme; veal with caramelized apricots and jewel-like prunes. These are inspired, delectable combinations.

One of the country's most important—and original—cooking methods is the *tagine*, a stew or ragout slow-cooked in an eponymous earthenware casserole with a conical lid.

The key is the lid, which captures the moisture rising from the cooking meat, poultry, or fish, and enables it to condense on the lid's walls, so that it can fall back onto the stew, keeping the dish moist while retaining its flavors.

Tagines frequently exhibit Moroccan cuisine's fond-ness for combining textures and marrying bold flavors, and showcase one of its distinguishing traits—the harmonious blending of sweet and savory. Take just two of countless examples: chicken topped with caramelized tomato compote and toasted almonds and veal shanks with stewed pears that carry a sweet freshness hinting of cloves, ginger, and cinnamon.

Knives are not found on Moroccan tables—tradition, sure, but also because they're not needed when meat cooks to the falling-off-the-bone tender-ness of a typical tagine. Yet as succulent as that lamb or beef or chicken might be, it sometimes seems that the sole purpose of a tagine is the final sauce, the rich melody of concentrated flavors mopped up with hunks of bread.

Couscous is another dish synonymous with Morocco and, like the tagine, is an ancient creation of the indigenous Berbers. The name refers to the dish as well as to the tiny "grains" made from hard durum wheat (or barley or even ground corn) that are double- or triple-steamed in a basket over simmer-ing, flavorful broth. This simple staple is turned into a traditional, celebrated centerpiece every Friday, when extended families gather around a shared platter of couscous for the week's most important meal. Topping the mound of tender couscous might be chicken and caramelized onions and raisins along with a scattering of crunchy almonds, seven different vegetables, or large pieces of pumpkin flavored with lamb. Typically served alongside are glasses of rich, slightly acidic buttermilk called *lben*.

Moroccan cuisine remains centered around such family meals. In a small village in the Ourika Valley, on the western slopes of the High Atlas, a young Berber woman explained to me how her family eats a tagine nearly every day, "It is placed in the center of the table for the whole family. One table, one dish. It is unacceptable to eat apart."

"Eating is not an individual experience," echoed a friend from the agricultural heartland between Fès and Marrakech. "Everyone is equal when eating. It's about sharing." Along with that sense of community over a meal, he continued, "there is a close connec-tion to the food. People usually eat with their [right] hand—using bread, making balls of couscous. It's about touching the food, feeling it."

For many, that connection begins by shopping—in the small markets along crowded lanes; from the butcher or fishmonger, the vendor of couscouses and flours, of olives and preserved lemons, of fresh herbs; from neighborhood *hanouts* (shops), often tiny but packed with a huge array of items on their shelves; or, in the large cities, in enormous supermarkets. Remaining strong, even vital, is the tradition of the weekly *souq* that gathers together fruits and vegetables, spices, livestock, and whatever else might be bought, sold, or traded. In the countryside, and especially at crossroads towns—Ouazzane in the north, Agdz in the Drâa Valley, Tiznit and Guelmim in the south—sprawling, weekly markets gather on the outskirts and draw thousands from the region to the selection of products brought in from the countryside: heaps of yellow melons dabbed with identifying markers of paint, papery purple red onions, clementines, boxes of sticky dates, mounds of small, pointed almonds and dried turmeric roots. There is an enclosed section for livestock—live sheep and goats, chicks and chickens, and in the south, at the famous Guelmim market, camels (not for transport, but meat).

Seafood is abundant in this meat-rich country. The lengthy seacoasts offer sardines, sea bream, turbot, sole, conger eel, mackerel, swordfish, and tuna, crab, shrimp, lobster, and oysters. Fish is often marinated in *charmoula*—a lively blend of fresh parsley and cilantro, garlic, cumin, sweet paprika, lemon juice, and olive oil—and then fried, cooked in a tagine, or stuffed with chopped tomatoes, fleshy violet-colored olives, and preserved lemons and baked. Grilled sardines are a coastal street food favorite. Generously sprinkled with sea salt and set just above embers, they're cooked for a couple of minutes on each side until the skin blackens and buckles, and devoured while barely cool enough to handle. The flavors are at their robust finest, the flesh sparkling and briny and shaded with smoky oils.

Rarely, though, are flavors as straightforward as grilled sardines. Moroccan cooks draw liberally from an ample spice box: ginger, saffron, cinnamon, and cumin are just four favorites among many. They blend

spices with finesse and use a generous hand with fresh herbs—parsley, cilantro, and mint. Aromatic *ma zhar* (orange flower water) and *ma ward* (rose water) are sprinkled on savory salads and sweet desserts, though often not until the end, so that none of their potent, evocative fragrance dissipates. Olives and preserved lemons add sassy tartness to salads, chicken tagines, and fish dishes, while toasted almonds and sesame seeds not only are main ingredients in many desserts, but offer salads, tagines, and couscouses a contrast of texture as well as a decorative element.

> In food, presentation remains of utmost importance. "First we eat with our eyes," says a Moroccan expression.

"You don't have to eat it all, but you can feast upon it with your eyes," justified one Moroccan friend as we faced an array of *fifteen* different salads at the start of a dinner. The ample amounts of food prepared are always generously offered, especially to guests. "Where two can eat so can ten." Who knows who might come while the family dines; and everyone will be welcomed. Tables are round—as opposed to square—and can much easier accommodate guests. There is always room for one more. (Weddings call for extra tables, just in case.)

There is a second meaning to that expression about eating first with the eyes, an ornamental one. It begins with the natural coloring of food—golds from saffron and turmeric, reds from sweet paprika and tomatoes—and ends in presentation. I have seen cooks not *just* add a piece of preserved lemon peel to a chicken tagine, but quarter it, trim the edges into a decorative shape—a serrated leaf, a flower blossom—and then lay it on top with the delicacy of gold flake. Or, with the most rustic Berber vegetable couscous, spend ten minutes ornately arranging strips of carrots, zucchini, and turnips on a massive mound of barley couscous grains and exactly positioning individual chickpeas around the base. Or stuff fat *mejhoul* dates not with *just* plain, pale-colored almond paste, but

first divide it, mix with some drops of red or green or blue food coloring before stuffing. But even that is still too plain. A walnut half is pressed into the top of the stuffed date before rolling it all in glistening sugar like crushed diamonds.

This attention paid to the eye even in the most straightforward dishes shows a respect for the skill (and effort) of the cook, for the products, and for the guests, as well as for the pleasure in the design element. It seems to me that this is in part due to the culture's highly developed sense of visual artistic expression, with the long tradition of arabesques, in repeating and interlacing patterns used for decoration—on walls, in carpets, covering ceramic *zellij* tile mosaics—and in the flowing forms in Arabic calligraphy.

"Food reveals a lot about people," Fabrizio Ruspoli, the dashing owner of the legendary restaurant and hotel La Maison Arabe in Marrakech, told me over a tray of intricate, honeyed pastries, mini masterpieces stuffed with crushed almonds and walnuts and speckled with ivory sesame seeds. "Look at the presentation. These are like little paintings, a joy to look at. Here they prepare to be pleasing to the palate—but also to the eye."

On another occasion, over a typical late, multi-course, and unhurried dinner, Fabrizio summed up the principles of Moroccan cooking: "Time to prepare, time to cook, time for the presentation." And then, with a playful smile, he added, "And, of course, time to eat and enjoy."

Although one can speak of a singular, unified "Moroccan cuisine," each region has its own variations and dishes that reflect its distinct geography, climate, influences, and history. Indeed, every dish in this book has roots, and those roots begin firmly in a region, village, or home.

Getting beyond the classic dishes from Fès and Marrakech that dominate most Moroccan cookbooks meant going to numerous different places that offered other angles on what "Moroccan cooking" means. Although I had traveled widely in Morocco during the past decade, for more than a year, while I wrote this book, I tried to spend a week or ten days every month in the country. I focused each trip on a particular region, hung out inside kitchens, snooped around *souqs* and shops, and ate versions of the same dishes in a diversity of places and types of locales. I tried to get an appreciation for similarities as well as differences, for what made each place special. From the Rif Mountains to the High Atlas, from coastal Asilah and Safi to the date-filled oasis of Zagora and the pre-Saharan market towns of Tiznit and Tan Tan, from rustic Berber cooking to the Spanish influences in the far north, the dizzyingly complex flavors worthy of the palace kitchen and the more straightforward tastes of the Sahara region celebrate the humble tagine as well as dishes calling for a dozen ingredients.

The more I traveled,
the more I realized that
Morocco has it all.

In kitchens across the country, I delighted in learning to make such sophisticated dishes as lamb tagine with oranges and saffron threads in Marrakech or, in Ouarzazate, poussin stuffed with almond and date paste, an exquisite pièce de résistance prepared for special celebrations. I took just as much pleasure in stuffing High Atlas Berber flatbread with freshly pulled shallots and pieces of the hard white fat that surrounds a lamb's kidney, a midmorning snack that kids typically carry warm to field workers to eat with glasses of sweet mint tea. Or—in Safi and El Jadida, and again in Essaouira—rolling hundreds of sardine balls that stewed in a pot of tomato sauce, an extremely popular dish that Moroccan families take along when they flock to the beach in summer. Each of these dishes is equally interesting—and representative.

"Food is the first stage in understanding [this place], the easiest way to get into it," a Berber woman from the Ourika Valley succinctly told me, "because it is so key to our culture." The goal of this book is to offer an appreciation of Moroccan cuisine—or, rather, *cuisines*—and a tasty way into a complex and fascinating culture.

A NOTE ON COOKING FROM THIS BOOK

"Ainek misanek" goes a Moroccan expression that roughly translates to "Your eye will be your measure." I've heard it often from Moroccan cooks in response to "How long?" "How much?" or "How many?" Spices differ in potency, flours absorb different amounts of water, one cut of meat might take a bit longer to become tender, medium heat on one stove is not the same as on another, and so on. And, of course, perceptions of taste differ from person to person. As a chef friend wisely told me some years ago, "The most important tool in the kitchen is your finger. Use it to taste frequently as you cook." Let that, and your eye, guide your measure.

A NOTE ON TRANSLITERATION

Writing Arabic words into the Latin alphabet generates numerous difficulties, no less so with Moroccan food terms. Each, it seems, has a half-dozen spelling variations. I have not adhered to one rigorous linguistic method, but used a couple different sources that best reflect what I have come across in the country, on packaging, on signs, in books—basically, what makes it easiest to travel, eat, shop, and get around in Morocco, and to navigate material in print and online about its cuisine. With the country's colonial past, transliteration generally follows a French phonetic system. For place-names, including Marrakech, Fès, and Tanger, that have accepted English spellings, I have used the form found on Google Maps and Michelin road maps that best reflects what is used in the country and by Moroccans. Note, as well, that the spelling of Berber words may alter slightly depending on the dialect.

A BRIEF
CULINARY HISTORY

Moroccan cuisine reflects the country's complex history and diversity of influences, from the ancient Berbers to those who have come and stayed, come and left, or just passed through—the Phoenicians and Romans, Arabs, Muslim and Jewish exiles from Andalucía, trans-Saharan caravans across the interior and Portuguese along the coast, English traders who introduced tea in the eighteenth century, and French and Spanish who ruled as colonial administrators in the twentieth. Each culture has left its mark.

BEGINNINGS

The country's storied past begins with the indigenous Berbers. A sizable percentage of the country's population today identify themselves as Berber, with many more having Berber ancestry. Berbers are found predominantly in the mountainous regions and the fringes of the Sahara, where they have retained their own language and customs while absorbing waves of influences. Great Berber dynasties once controlled not only Morocco but south into western Africa and north into Spain.

The name *Berber* possibly derives from a Greek and Roman expression referring to those who did not speak the Greek or Roman language, and was later popularized in other languages. While the name has lost its pejorative connotations (the same root spawned *barbarian*), many Berbers prefer to call themselves *Imazighen* (or *similar*, depending on the dialect), which means "free men" or "noble men." Berbers are not a homogenous people, and their language has three main dialects: Tachelhaït, in the southwest, the High Atlas, Drâa Valley, and Souss; Tamazight, in the Middle Atlas; and Tarifit (or Riffi), in the Rif Mountains. "But we have many shared characteristics," one High Atlas Berber explained to me. "A shared history, the same roots, similar characters in many respects, lifestyles, food…"

Berber cuisine remains generally rustic, sometimes almost frugal, reflecting the often harsh conditions and austere landscape where they live, but also a deep history that was once nomadic and seminomadic, with little time for various courses or flourish. They might have settled, but the ancestral cuisine remains. Grains, legumes, and vegetables continue to be mainstays of the diet. "We are largely vegetarian not by choice but by poverty," a man in one arid valley wryly told me. But Berbers are credited with developing some of Morocco's most prominent dishes, including the tagine and couscous, which they call *sksou*. Berber versions of these dishes are, not surprisingly, typically hearty with vegetables (and flavored with a bit of lamb or beef, even turkey) and show little of the complex seasoning found in other, more urban places like Fès.

Berbers are also credited with two national comfort foods, the smooth, tomato-based soup called *harira* (page 73) and *bessara*, a purée of fava beans thinned into soup and spiced with cumin and paprika and served with olive oil (see page 77), as well as strips of preserved meat called *khlea* (page 44). They are also known for a number of interesting flatbreads, including a layered one called *rghayif* (page 64) that is eaten with honey.

The *moussem*, or saints' day celebration, often celebrated around a pilgrimage to a mausoleum, remains important. These celebrations are firstly religious and secondly social and commercial, and involve days of music, dancing, and festivities, with the rather exuberant Berber character coming through. In verdant areas abundant with flocks of grazing sheep, the centerpiece of the feast is often a whole spit-roasted lamb, or *mechoui* (page 121), surely one of the country's greatest culinary experiences. Some of the more high-spirited *moussems* are in Tan Tan, famous for its camel and horse fantasia that gathers numerous nomadic Saharan tribes together, one based around the rose harvest in the Anti-Atlas town of El Kelâa des M'Gouna, and in Moulay Idriss in the hills above Meknès.

PHOENICIANS, ROMANS, AND THE EARLY INVADERS

Morocco has a number of Phoenician and Roman settlements. Along the coast, ancient Punic colonies or city-states—namely Lixus (near modern-day Larache), Tingis (Tanger), Chellah (Rabat), Mogador (Essaouira)—brought advances in farming and agriculture techniques, and settlers planted olives, vines, and fruit orchards. After the fall of Carthage (in modern-day Tunisia) in 146 BCE, Rome secured its influence in the region, established Roman North Africa, and ruled from the Nile to the Atlantic across the top of the continent. In Morocco, Romans rebuilt the city of Volubilis (outside Meknès), expanded wheat and olive production and vineyards, and produced their beloved fermented fish paste called *garum*. These foods helped feed the vast Roman Empire until its collapse at the end of the fifth century. It's also likely that during their time in the area, Romans introduced cooking in clay vessels, which Berbers later adapted into tagines.

ARABS

After the death of the prophet Muhammad in 632 CE, Islam swept westward from the Arabian Peninsula through the Middle East and Egypt and into North Africa by the beginning of the eighth century. Along with a new religion (and its dietary restrictions), a new language, a new model of government, and a sophisticated level of culture, the Arabs brought spices from the east—cinnamon, nutmeg, ginger, turmeric—and gradually introduced Persian and Arabic cooking influences. These included cooking meats with sweet fruit, using a mixture of spices as well as aromatics, a fondness for using nuts in cooking, and a passion for delicate sweetmeats with almonds, honey, and sesame seeds. Almost immediately, the Arabs established the great city of Fès, the heart of Morocco's Arabic—as opposed to Berber—culture.

The Muslim conquest continued on to the Iberian peninsula in 711 and in a decade had penetrated into France. (Muslim rule gradually shrank southward over the next 750 years.) Al-Andalus, as Muslim Spain and Portugal was known, was a sophisticated, cosmopolitan meeting place of the Orient and Occident where the art of cooking reached lofty heights. The region would be interlinked with Morocco until the final collapse of Muslim rule on the Iberian peninsula at the end of the fifteenth century.

IMPERIAL MOROCCO

Under a succession of imperial Berber dynasties, the region gradually moved from a patchwork of states into a unified entity with a sense of identity. The Almoravid Empire (1062–1145) stretched at its peak north into Spain, east to Algiers, and far south into what is today Mauritania, Mali, and northern Senegal, some 2,000 mi/3,200 km from north to south. Perhaps, though, its greatest accomplishment was founding Marrakech. The Almohad Empire (1145–1248) showed Morocco at its most potent, controlling territory that reached north into Spain, south into Mauritania, and east all the way across modern-day Algeria, Tunisia, and Libya. The Marinid Empire (1248–1465), though lacking the vast geographic range of its predecessors, managed to hold Morocco together for nearly two hundred years from its base in the great medieval city Fès. An Arab dynasty, for the first time, took control in the mid-sixteenth century. The Saadians (1554–1659) traced their lineage back to the prophet Muhammad, as do their successors, the Alaouites (1665–), who remain in power today. Both began their consolidation of power in the south, at the fringes of the desert with access to the trans-Saharan trade routes.

This was also the age of the great Saharan caravans that traveled north from Mali, Ghana, and Senegal with gold, slaves, cloth, and spices, and carried salt in the other direction. The peak of the trans-Saharan trade lasted from the eighth century until the end of the sixteenth century, with the collapse of the great Songhai Empire in West Africa and trade shifting more to the Atlantic. (Railroads at the beginning of the twentieth century and Land Rovers essentially smothered out what remained.) Goods carried on ancient caravans of long columns of laden camels passed through oasis towns like Sijilmasa (in the Tafilalt oasis, but today merely ruins) to Marrakech, Fès, and Meknès, to Tanger, and onto

Mediterranean Europe, where the demand for gold coinage was nearly insatiable. Those in Morocco called the area to the south Bilad al-Sudan, "the Land of the Blacks." The name refers not to the modern-day country of Sudan, but to the geographic region stretching across North Africa from the Atlantic to the Nile, from the southern edge of the Sahara to the tropical equatorial region. A handful of products retain the legacy of this African trade in their names, most prominently hot red pepper, *felfla soudaniya*, or often just called *soudaniya*.

RECONQUISTA AND (RE)SETTLING

Almost immediately after the eighth-century invasion of Spain began the long and steady Catholic *reconquista*, a gradual process that ended in 1492 with the fall of Granada. When Spanish rulers expelled Muslims—after Granada's fall, and then with edicts over the next few centuries—many headed south to North Africa. Historians figure that some 800,000 Andalusians settled in Morocco, where they added new "Andalusian" neighborhoods to cities such as Fès, and built whole new cities such as Chefchaouen or Tétouan, which they rebuilt over ruins. The refugees brought with them the Arabic-Berber (sometimes called Moorish) flavors that had been refined and heightened in Spain. These can be tasted in, for instance, the blending of the sweet and savory (or even sour), certain spice mixes, and ways of preserving fruits.

JEWS

Expelled from Spain along with Muslims, many Jews immigrated to Morocco. Although their presence in Morocco dates to Roman North Africa in the early centuries of the Common Era, various large waves of these immigrants from Spain made the greatest impact. Controlling much of the trade of Morocco's two great commodities—sugar and salt—they often lived in *mellahs*, Jewish residential quarters. *Mellah* comes from the Arabic word for "salt." Some historians think this name originated not with the role of Jewish immigrants as salt traders but with the salty stream running through Fès' Jewish quarter, or even with the community's onetime role in salting the heads of executed criminals to display on city walls.

The Moroccan Jewish community was once formidable. A 1936 census counted 161,942 Jews in the country. By 1948—the peak—the Jewish population is generally given as 265,000, with flourishing communities in Fès and Marrakech, in the coastal cities of Casablanca, Rabat, Essaouira, and Safi, and inland in Tiznit, where Jewish craftspeople were renowned for their silver jewelry. That year, with the creation of Israel, the first exodus left the country. Another wave departed in 1963, once the suspension on emigration (enacted with independence in 1956) was lifted, and more followed with the 1967 Arab-Israeli War. Perhaps fewer than five thousand remain today, with most living in Casablanca.

Many traditional Jewish dishes were lost when the community left, such as *dafina*, a spicy-sweet stew traditionally cooked on the Sabbath with calves' foot and tongue, dumplings, and dates. A handful of dishes have been integrated, however, and are not considered strictly Jewish today, including *hargma*, a popular stew of calves' feet and chickpeas. Jewish influence can also be seen in ways of preserving foods and in some pastries.

EUROPEAN INFLUENCE

In the fifteenth and sixteenth centuries, the Portuguese punctuated the Atlantic coast with a number of fortified ports, including Tanger, Asilah, Anfa (now Casablanca), Azemmour, Mazagan (now El Jadida), Safi, Essaouira, and Agadir. They sought direct trade from south of the Sahara for gold, and coastal outlets that would allow them to avoid the Genoese dominance of Mediterranean maritime trade. They also wanted to tap into Morocco's rich lands of cereals and fish.

In 1830, France took control of neighboring Algiers from the Ottomans, who had ruled since 1520. With the exception of the northeastern border city of Oujda, Morocco was able to hold them at bay until the early twentieth century. French occupation began in 1907 with Casablanca, and in 1912 the country was partitioned into two Protectorates governed individually by France and Spain, with Tanger designated an international zone. France ruled the majority of the country from its new capital in Rabat. The French built ports in Casablanca and Kénitra and new towns in Rabat, Fès, Meknès, Marrakech, and elsewhere, largely leaving the ancient medinas untouched. They introduced baguettes among flatbreads and morning croissants among *rghayif* (page 64); a slightly different version of café culture, with the terraces sprawled out on wide, *ville nouvelle* boulevards; and a wine industry.

Spain's early impact in Morocco came in the Mediterranean coastal enclaves of Melilla and Ceuta, which Spain held beginning in the fifteenth century. Under the Protectorate, Spain ruled the Mediterranean north of the country, with Tétouan as its capital, until the 1956 independence. For a large part of the twentieth century, Spain also controlled the deep south with the colony of the Sáhara Occidental (Western Sahara, until 1976), the Tarfaya Strip to its north (until 1958), and the beach town of Sidi Ifni (until 1969).

The lingering Spanish influence remains clearest in the north, where tomatoes and paprika are more widespread in the cooking than in the south, and where fish is frequently fried *without* a spicy marinade. Today, many Moroccan immigrants to Spain come from the north. When they return—to spend their holidays or to live—they bring with them a new layer of influence.

INDEPENDENT MOROCCO

Morocco became independent in 1956 and has been led by a series of kings—Mohammed V, Hassan II, and, since 1999, Mohammed VI.

During the centuries of imperial rule, royal kitchens have ensured a high-level consciousness of the culinary arts. In 1979, King Hassan II set up a royal cooking school on the grounds of the palace in Rabat. It continues to run and each year accepts forty Moroccan girls under twenty-five years of age (many from the countryside) for the two-year program. The girls are trained in the high art of classical Moroccan cooking by sheer repetition.

Morocco continues to assimilate influences in the kitchen while keeping its unique culinary identity. A recent, important influence is a woman known as Choumicha. One of the best-known personalities in the country, Choumicha has become something of a culinary media empire, with books, TV programs,

and, for a time, a cooking magazine. On TV, she prepares traditional recipes with elderly women around the country and also adapts Moroccan dishes for a modern, more time-pressed audience. She has published a large, lovely cookbook, though it's her small, inexpensive booklets with recipes focusing on a single theme such as tagines or desserts that are hugely popular with Moroccans.

For many years, travelers heard that to eat well in Morocco, to eat authentic Moroccan cuisine, they had to dine in a private home, something that is difficult for the casual visitor. But that has happily changed with the explosion of *riads*—a style of house that opens to a courtyard, and now refers to a small bed-and-breakfast, with just a couple of rooms, in the medina. A local cook or two prepare meals for a handful of clients, using ingredients bought in the neighborhood markets, and the meals are frequently served family style. The experience feels like being a privileged guest in a private home.

And there is the surprising, and welcome, trend of very good, inexpensive eateries in gas stations along motorways and on the edges of towns. At many Petromin, Baraka, Petrom, Afriquia, and Shell stations across the country, rows of tagines slow-cook on embers while freshly made flatbreads bake in traditional earthen ovens. You can tell the best ones by the number of cars in the parking lot.

International supermarkets can be found on the outskirts of larger cities, with Marjane (considered the best), Carrefour, Acima, and a local chain called Aswak Assalam offering both local products and imported ones, usually from Europe.

The culinary mosaic continues. To grow, sure, but also to be more accessible.

A COOK'S TOUR
OF THE LAND

Morocco is, in a sense, an island, surrounded on the west by the Atlantic Ocean and on the north by the Mediterranean Sea, and on the east and south by the pre-Sahara and Sahara Desert. Within its ample borders, a wide variety of geographical features can be found: mountain ranges, mesas and oases, deserts, river valleys, and fertile coastal fishing grounds. In 1975, Morocco's landmass expanded greatly—from 172,414 sq mi/446,550 sq km, or slightly bigger than California, to 274,460 sq mi/710,850 sq km—when it annexed the southern Sahara region previously controlled by Spain. The country's population stands at around 34 million, with a majority living in cities along the northern and central Atlantic coastline, and in Fès and Marrakech. The rest of the country remains largely rural.

Morocco's history has given cooks the inspiration and tools to develop one of the world's richest cuisines, and the country's vast and varied landscape offers all the raw materials needed.

Dakhla ✕

MEDITERRANEAN

Tanger ✗   ✗ Tétouan

Asilah ✗
        ✗ Chefchaouen

ATLANTIC OCEAN   RIF
                    MOUNTAINS   Oujda ✗

            Salé ✗
    Rabat ✗   Meknès   ✗ Fès
Casablanca ✗   ✗
        ✗ Azemmour   Azrou ✗
El Jadida ✗
                                        MIDDLE ATLAS
Oualidia ✗

    Safi ✗
            HIGH ATLAS

Essaouira ✗   Marrakech ✗
                                        Erfoud ✗
                    Ouarzazate ✗   DRÂA
                                          RIVER
            Taliouine ✗   Agdz ✗
Agadir ✗   Zagora ✗
                            Mhamid ✗
        ✗ Tiznit
                ANTI-ATLAS
Sidi Ifni ✗   SAHARA
        ✗ Guelmim

Tan Tan Plage ✗✗ Tan Tan

    ✗ Tarfaya

✗ Laâyoune
        ✗ Smara

SAHARA

TANGER, TÉTOUAN, AND
THE NORTHWEST TIP

In close proximity to Spain and Europe, and strad-
dling the Atlantic Ocean and the Mediterranean Sea,
the northern triangular tip of Morocco is the most
hybrid part of the country. Spain lies in sight across
the Strait of Gibraltar, just 9 mi/14 km wide at its
narrowest. This is Europe and Africa's meeting point, a
place showing Spanish influences—lightly floured and
fried fish and calamari (see page 158), rice dishes,
a love of sweet, smoked paprika—yet still holding a
clear North African personality. Cooks might first
bathe fish in plenty of zesty *charmoula* marinade and
then stuff it with plump olives and preserved lemons
as well as rice.

At the point of the tip is Tanger, the oldest
continually inhabited city in the country. A place of
legends and myths, the city retains a heady blend

of influences from all those who have controlled it:
Phoenicians (who founded the city around 1100 BCE),
Romans, Byzantines, Visigoths, Arabs, Portuguese,
and British (who were there for a short time in the
seventeenth century). Tanger's status as an international city from the 1920s to the 1950s brought more
modern, cosmopolitan influences.

About 30 mi/48 km south down the Atlantic
coast is the Portuguese-built port of Asilah, with
its tight, whitewashed seaside medina resplendent
in brilliant blue doors and shutters. On weekends,
families flock to small restaurants for fresh fish and
calamari fried in the light Andalusian style—using
just flour and a bit of salt. Platters come with a dish
of puréed tomato dipping sauce and stack of fresh
bread. Diners eat directly on paper place mats, then
fold the picked-clean bones and shells into the place
mats and throw them away.

An hour southeast of Tanger lies Tétouan, whose dense tiers of low, whitewashed houses spread up a valley of orange, almond, and pomegranate orchards from the Mediterranean. The city was largely built in the fifteenth and sixteenth centuries by Muslim and Jewish refugees from Spain. It is known in Arabic as "white dove" and "daughter of Granada." Tétouanese architecture, mosaic tile work, music, jewelry, and refined cooking are impregnated with Andalusian heritage. You can taste it in the honeyed onion and raisin *tfaya* (see page 166) that tops tagines and couscouses; in *seffa* (page 205), sweet couscous with raisins and almonds; and in crispy, paper-thin sheets of pastry interspersed with ground almonds, sugar, and cinnamon.

The history of Tétouan has continued to intertwine with that of Spain. In the seventeenth and eighteenth centuries, the city's strategic location and cultural ties formed a bridge between Morocco and Spain—and Europe. During those prosperous centuries, all of Morocco's trade to Europe passed through Tétouan. When Morocco became a Protectorate, the Spanish named Tétouan the capital of the section under their control.

Eastern flavors are discernible in Tétouan, too. After Ottoman-ruled Algiers fell into the hands of the French in 1830, Tétouan became home to generations of Algerian immigrants. They brought with them Turkish and Middle Eastern influences in grilling meat and skewers of seasoned, ground *kefta* (see page 94) directly over embers, in using milk in desserts like the lovely pudding called *m'halbi* (see page 198), and in preparing such favorite sweetmeats as sugarcoated gazelle-horn cookies, baklava, and *m'hancha*, coiled "serpentine" pastry stuffed with almond paste.

THE RIF MOUNTAINS

Beginning east of Tétouan and running 200 mi/320 km along the northern Mediterranean coastline, the Rif Mountains form a protective arc of largely impenetrable limestone and sandstone that crests up sharply from the sea to 8,200 ft/2,500 m. Cedar, cork, holm oak, and pine and a medley of wildflowers coat the hills. Home to the Riffian Berbers, the area is one of the most isolated parts of the country.

It was here in the fifteenth century that Andalusian refugees built the blue-hued city of Chefchaouen. Due to the city's isolation, defensive position slotted between two summits, holy status, and rabid anti-foreignism that lasted until the 1920s, the area has seemingly changed little, and its strong and distinct identity remains largely preserved. The pine-filled hills around Chefchaouen are dense with olive, almond, plum, and fig orchards, as well as thirty-five varieties of edible wild mushrooms. The rustic cooking of the countryside relies heavily on local herbs, fragrant honeys, and herds of goats whose milk Riffian Berbers make into pungent cheeses and whose meat they stew in tagines (see page 122). Few dishes are as homey and hearty as the beloved *bessara*, a puréed soup of dried and split fava beans or split peas with cumin and paprika and served with a drizzle local olive oil (see page 77).

FÈS, MEKNÈS, AND THE MIDDLE ATLAS

Fès is the country's oldest Imperial City, its symbolic heart and traditional culinary capital. As a Fassi—a resident of Fès—from one of the city's noble families proudly told me, "When we talk about Morocco, we talk about Fès." Founded in the last years of the eighth century by the Arabs, who had swept into Morocco shortly before then, Fès was the religious, trade, and cultural center of the country until the French moved the capital to Rabat in 1912. It was here in this dense, quiet, and often private city—especially compared to the open and lively squares of cities like Marrakech—that the concept of "Morocco" took hold and, by extension, "Moroccan cuisine."

Fès was a crossroads, a stopping point, and even a destination for the great caravans of the past that came from each corner of the country, from Andalucía, the Sahara, the Middle East. The *souqs*

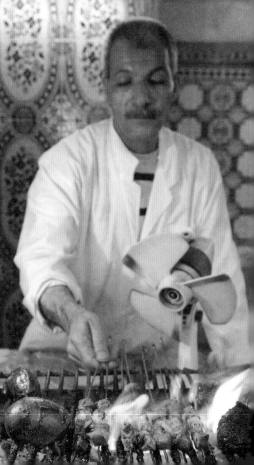

of the extensive medieval medina—containing a staggering 9,500 narrow alleys, lanes, and passageways—offer all that even the most discerning cook could possibly desire. Even today, someone coming from elsewhere in Morocco immediately notices the ampleness of choice, the more varieties of flour, of legumes, of honey.

It's no surprise, then, that Fassi cooking is generally considered the most sophisticated in Morocco, a product of Arab, Andalusian, and Jewish roots; extreme pride; and abundant local foodstuffs.

Influences came, too, from desert oases. These supplied goods, but also cooks and workers, as well. With their valuable water that drew travelers and settlers and also watered date palms, they were a great source of wealth. The culinary arts have long held a place of prestige here. Spices are mixed with particular refinement, the sweet and savory blended with unparalleled sublimity and harmony, and the presentation is exacting.

A number of Fassi dishes remain particularly memorable: the famous stuffed pastry *pastilla* with squab or chicken; a "sweet" tagine topped with stewed tomatoes caramelized with honey, perfumed with a few delicate drops of orange flower water or rose water, and scattered with toasted almonds and sesame seeds (see page 144); a savory chicken tagine called *khdra* with plenty of onions and almonds in the buttery saffron sauce (see page 147). There is pleasure, too, in the simpler street foods of the medina, including the beloved stuffed spleen (*tihane* or *rate farcie*), the deep-fried potato fritters called *maakouda* (see page 83), and the hard spring plums pickled in brine, sold in candy stores and by kids who carry plastic tubs of the plums prepared by their mothers.

Just forty-five minutes west of Fès lies the low-key and overshadowed Imperial City of Meknès. With olive and citrus groves and fields of some of the country's finest mint surrounding the city, it is no surprise that Meknès has a celebrated covered market filled with neat, geometric displays of preserved olives and lemons and abundant fresh herbs. The land around Meknès is also home to vineyards. The burgeoning wine industry is laid over the foundations of French viticulture from the Protectorate era and, to an extent, the Roman tradition around the nearby ancient city of Volubilis. The largest winemaker is Les Celliers de Meknès, with nearly 5,000 acres/2,000 ha of vineyards.

To the south of these two cities begins the Middle Atlas, a range pockmarked with volcanic peaks, etched by river gorges, and covered in oak, cork, ash, juniper, and stands of giant cedar trees that reach up to 130 ft/40 m. The northwestern slope of the range irrigates the oranges, lemons, and olives of Meknès, the artichokes and wild cardoon thistles of Fès, and the cherries of Sefrou, while the southern slope carries water to the orchards of apples, apricots, plums, and walnuts around Midelt.

The Berber city of Azrou, the first of the important Middle Atlas towns south from Fès or Meknès, has fruit orchards and honey, and is well known for its trout, which once swam wild in its streams. The French established trout pisciculture in the first half of the twentieth century during the Protectorate and raised the fish in the cool hills away from the heat of the plains. Area cooks prepare the trout in the French-influenced meunière sauce or in their own, distinctive ways—panfried and sprinkled with crushed almonds or, my favorite, stuffed with grated carrots, fresh bay leaves, and plenty of black pepper (see page 163).

The lush hills of the Middle Atlas are famous for their fertile grazing land for sheep as well as for their wild herbs, which find their way into teas and infusions, traditional medicines, and many savory dishes. In Azrou, for instance, cooks include fresh mint in their ground meat *kefta* (see page 94). Another area well known for its herbs is around Taza, the citadel city that guards the Taza Gap between the Middle Atlas and the Rif Mountains and the eastern entrance to Fès.

Farther east, at the reaches of these ranges near the Algerian border, is Oujda, the capital of the Oriental Region, the only city in modern-day Morocco to have been occupied by the Ottomans. Turkish rule lasted from 1727 until the early 1800s.

THE ATLANTIC COAST FROM RABAT TO AGADIR AND SOUTH

Morocco's Atlantic coast stretches from the fertile, populous north all the way to the dry, sparsely populated south where the Sahara meets the sea.

The northern part holds the cosmopolitan cities of Rabat and Casablanca. The French named Rabat the country's capital at the beginning of the Protectorate in 1912, and it remained so after independence in 1956. The youngest of Morocco's four Imperial Cities, Rabat is known to the epicurean for its sweet dishes and dried fruits. Seven Vegetable Couscous (page 180)— Morocco's national dish—and couscous topped with the caramelized onion and raisin *tfaya* (see page 166) are extremely popular in Rabat as well as in Salé, the capital's more conservative neighbor just across the mouth of the Bou Regreg River. Salé also has a

wonderful lamb dish with coriander seeds called *mkila* (see page 120) that is as robustly savory as *tfaya* is sweet.

An hour to the south is Casablanca, Morocco's business capital. Although it has grown from a village of 20,000 in 1906 to a heaving metropolis of about 3.5 million today (one-tenth of the country's population), it remains steeped in tradition. The city offers not only magnificent seafood restaurants along La Corniche, the lovely waterfront promenade, but in many minds bests Rabat in its love for, and skill in preparing, seven vegetable couscous.

South of Casablanca, the Atlantic coast turns wild and windy, with great sweeps of undeveloped beach and rocky cliffs, along with crashing surf. Punctuating the coastline are a handful of fishing ports protected by centuries-old ramparts— Azemmour, El Jadida, Oualidia, Safi, Essaouira.

The sea swarms with turbot, sole, bream, mackerel, swordfish, blue shark, conger eel, tuna, shrimp, lobster, crab, and even oysters. The last are a specialty of Oualidia, where beds were arranged in the 1950s in a long, thin, sheltered lagoon.

But it's a small, silvery fish that dominates Morocco's fishing industry: the humble *serdine* (sardine). Morocco is the world's largest producer and exporter, with fleets based in Safi, El Jadida, Essaouira, Agadir, and Tan Tan Plage (El Ouatia). Plants in Safi process hundreds of thousands of tons of sardines a year, but not all the catch goes into tins. Fresh sardines remain the country's most popular, and economical, fish. Many families eat them weekly and in a variety of ways—filleted and ground with herbs and spices, rolled into marble-size balls, and stewed in a fragrant tomato sauce (see page 160); stewed whole with fresh fava beans; cooked in a

tagine over a bed of sliced potatoes and plum tomatoes. On the street, whole sardines are grilled over embers (see page 91), or coupled pairs of butterflied fillets are rubbed with a garlic and herb paste and then deep-fried (see page 88).

In Essaouira, where seagulls wheel over the city's eighteenth-century ramparts, cooks prepare fish tagines, especially conger eel with caramelized onions. Conger is flavorful, but monkfish is a preferred, though more expensive option (see page 166). The city has an important heritage from Moroccan Jews, who, at the beginning of the twentieth century, made up perhaps half of the city's population.

South of Agadir, the Anti-Atlas erupts, and long stretches of the coast are rocky and inhospitable, broken with cliffs and rolling surf, and hold just a handful of isolated settlements, namely Mirleft and Sidi Ifni. Spain controlled the latter from 1476 to 1542,

calling it Santa Cruz del Mar Pequeño, and again from 1860 until 1969. The buildings feature art deco curves, and the market is full of seafood—sardines, calamari, and, unusually in Morocco, mussels. Mussels are cooked in tagines (see page 154) and also stewed in a tomato sauce that is nearly identical to a Spanish *sofrito*, with purely Moroccan additions of cumin and cilantro (see page 153). Inland, prickly pear cacti coat the hills, and women's co-ops have begun making marmalade from the fruit.

From here south through Tan Tan and where the Drâa Valley meets the sea begins the Sahara. Fishermen perch on high cliffs, casting for bream and croaker, and at low tide scramble down to the waterline to collect mussels as well as *percebes*, goose barnacles with soft black bodies and hard, clawlike shells, for export to Spain.

MARRAKECH AND THE HIGH ATLAS

At a strategic transit point on the north side of the High Atlas lies Marrakech, the great Berber city founded in 1070 and capital of several powerful dynasties. Fringed in orange, lemon, and olive groves, infused with dazzling light, it feels overwhelmingly southern. Whereas the color of north is blue—*zellij* tiles in Tanger and Tétouan, the walls in Chefchaouen, the paint on wooden sardine boats, the sea itself—here the color is pink, which glows warmly on the city walls. About 12 mi/19 km of thick, reddish pink clay ramparts, some 30 ft/9 m high, wrap around Marrakech. Begun in the 1120s, extended over the following centuries, and punctuated by two hundred towers and twenty gates, the walls protect the city's ancient heart—its medina and *souqs*, dense neighborhoods, palaces and tombs of ancient rulers, mosques and madrasahs (Qur'anic schools), and iconic square, Djemaa el Fna. Marrakech is Fès' only real rival as the country's culinary capital.

Marrakech cooking is rich, spicy but not hot, refined, and diverse. Culinary trademarks include lamb tagines with vegetables and fruits grown in the surrounding Haouz region and heavily spiced with red and black pepper, cumin, turmeric, saffron, and plenty of *ras el hanout* blended from dozens of ingredients.

One succulent Marrakech specialty is *tangia* (see page 129), named for the two-handled earthen urn used to prepare it. Packed with seasoned beef or lamb, crushed garlic, preserved lemon, and plenty of spices, the pot is sealed with a piece of thick paper and left to cook slowly for a number of hours in the embers of a *hammam* (steam bath) under the eye of the *farnachi*, the man who controls the fire.

The city's rather open character and appetite emerge as dusk falls and hundreds of stalls assemble on Djemaa el Fna among snake charmers, acrobats, and drummers, storytellers, henna painters, and healers from the Sahara hawking ancient aphrodisiac concoctions.

Clouds of grill smoke envelope the locals, tourists, Berbers down from the hills, and nomads from the desert who pack the stalls seeking skewers of grilled *kefta* or cubes of liver enveloped in *crépine* (white, veiny caul fat); finger-size *merguez*, spicy lamb sausages; bowls of tripe stew; soupy lentils (see page 78); and silky *harira* soup (see page 73). Snails served in a rich, digestive bouillon flavored with more than a dozen herbs and spices, including licorice, orange peel, ginger, cloves, and gunpowder green tea leaves (see page 85), remain a trademark dish.

Visible to the south and east of the city are the snowcapped peaks of the High Atlas. Stretching some 450 mi/724 km northeast from coastal Agadir toward Algeria, spreading 40 mi/64 km in width, and rising to 13,671 ft/4,167 m, the High Atlas is the grandest of Morocco's four mountain ranges. These slopes, with their flattop villages made of rocks, rammed earth *pisé*, and adobe bricks, and their beefy, fortified *agadirs* (collective granaries), are a Berber heartland.

CENTRAL MOROCCO
AND THE ANTI-ATLAS

Over the lofty, serpentine passes of the High Atlas, the land drops down, along streams and through terraced fields of barley that shimmer silvery green in spring and early summer, and into the rock-strewn Anti-Atlas range and sub-Sahara. The vast landscape of winnowed valleys opens out, with the occasional mud-and-straw *ksar* (fortified village) or crenellated towered *kasbah* (fortified house) blending into the ocher red earth. A handful of narrow rivers spread like veins, and a bright green ribbon of crops runs through the creases of naked hills, offering surprising riches.

From its headwaters in the High Atlas, the Drâa River drops east toward the desert before making a wide arc southwest, traversing the feet of the Anti-Atlas and then heading across the desert. There, apart from exceptionally wet years, the river dries and seeps into the parched earth in places before reaching the Atlantic just north of the desert port of Tan Tan Plage (El Ouatia). At 700 mi/1,125 km in length, it's the country's longest river.

Long before its outlet to the sea, just after it comes out of the mountains, the river gives birth to a fertile 80-mi/130-km riverine oasis, a string of date palm groves and villages from Agdz to past Zagora. The groves are broken by a labyrinth of high, thick earthen walls that shelter small green fields—with wheat or fruit trees (fig, apricot, pomegranate) under the shade of tall palm trees that produce some of the country's finest dates. Small paths weave through the dizzying maze, and saddled donkeys remain the most useful and common means of carrying the harvested fruit and dates. Important in terms of providing a source of wealth from crops and a strategic location near the trans-Saharan trade routes, the Drâa was the starting point for the Saadian dynasty in controlling Morocco.

On the north side of the Drâa runs the Dadès Valley. At the town of El Kelâa des M'Gouna begins the so-called Vallée des Roses, a tangle of dry valleys covered in low hedges that, in spring, blossom with small pink roses. These fragrant blossoms are distilled into the ubiquitous *ma ward* (rose water).

To the south of the Drâa, the area of Taliouine on the high Souktana plateau grows saffron, perhaps first brought to Moroccan shores thousands of years ago by Phoenician traders. In autumn, at dawn, whole families work together to harvest the flowers and then remove the precious stigmas. Used in countless dishes for its natural golden coloring and its distinctive flavor, the fragrant, valuable spice even laces tea (see page 211)—sometimes with fresh mint, sometimes instead of it.

Farther south, beyond the high peaks, and catching the moist sea breezes, the Souss Valley is the land of the leathery, spiny argan tree. Deep-rooted, sprawling, and living for up to a few centuries, the trees bear a greasy, olivelike fruit collected in summer.

Berber women extract the argan kernels, roast them, and then laboriously grind them on a rough stone mortar to extract a sand-colored, nutty-flavored oil that they drizzle over whole-grain bread, salads, and couscous.

They also blend the oil with the area's dark honey and small, crunchy almonds from the nearby Ameln Valley to make a thick dip called *amlou* (see page 199), which is eaten with hunks of fresh flatbread for breakfast or a snack.

THE SAHARA AND THE DEEP SOUTH

The eastern part of Morocco edges Algeria and the Sahara. These fringes hold the great oases and strategic trading posts along the ancient trans-Saharan caravan routes—Rissani, Tafilalt, Erfoud, Mhamid, Guelmim, Smara. Their shady palm groves provide sweet dates that are given to guests as a traditional welcome and are eaten as snacks and with fruit at the end of a meal. Dates are also stuffed *with* almond paste (see page 193) and are stuffed *into* young pigeons (see page 137), as well as used to decorate sweet couscous (see page 205).

The deep south, bordered by Algeria and Mauritania and by the long seacoast, was for the first seven decades of the twentieth century a Spanish colony. Integrated into Morocco in the mid-1970s, the sparsely populated area is largely made up of a pale, bleak stony desert called *hamada*; thorny scrubland with patches of ivory, yellowish, and ocher sand; and *oueds* (dried riverbeds) feathered with isolated tamarisk or acacia trees.

It is here that the Sahara meets the Atlantic. Inundated salt pans called *sabkhat* stretch for dozens of miles, glistening white and pink in the desert light. Although there are some coastal dunes, most often the land meets the sea in cliffs where fishermen perch and cast down with long rods into the pounding surf. The waters off Laâyoune and, another 330 mi/530 km farther south, Dakhla have some of the richest fishing beds in the entire region and supply markets not only in Morocco but in Europe and beyond.

The cooking of the deep south differs from that of the rest of the country. The markets have fewer offerings, and dishes tend to have sparser seasoning. Cooks use the meat of dromedary—the iconic one-humped camel—for grilling and stewing, and for grinding and forming into small patties cooked on a grill. The ancient Saturday *souq* on the outskirts of Guelmim, long famed for its camels, still sells them, though not for transport anymore but for food. So important is camel as a food that the camel *souq* is a daily event, whereas the general *souq* takes place only one day each week. The animals graze along the flat scrublands in the distance under the gaze of a lone shepherd. At butchers' stalls in towns, camel is the most common meat. For many of the region's traditionally nomadic people—women in their colorful wraps, men in pale turquoise robes detailed with golden thread—camel is one of the three main elements of their diet, along with dates and milk.

And tea! Three small glasses of mint tea—a dark, potent brew here, far from the delicate, aromatic, amber tones of, say, Fès—are drunk at a time, and remain an important tradition.

Atlas
plastic's
Atlas
plastic's
SIN CONSERVADORES NI COLORANTES
L'OLIVE ET LES CONDIMENTS

THE MOROCCAN PANTRY

Understanding a cuisine begins with its ingredients. Whether you are shopping for ingredients outside the country or in the *souqs* and *hanouts* (small shops) inside it, this compendium of herbs, spices, and other essentials, as well as kitchen tools, will help guide you.

In most cases, I have followed the English name with the French (**FR**) and Moroccan Arabic (**MOR**). In some cases where an ingredient is widely associated with Berbers, I have also given the Berber name.

As noted on page 11, I have used a number of sources for the spelling of Moroccan words. For herbs and spices, I followed Abdelhaï Sijelmassi's authoritative *Les plantes médicinales du Maroc* and, for date varieties, Hasnaâ Harrak and Abdelaziz Chetto's *Valorisation et commercialisation des dattes au Maroc*.

Note that the suffix *beldi* means "from the country" (local or Moroccan) and that *roumi*, from the word for *Roman*, means "from outside." Although not all local products carry these designations, some do for emphasis. For instance, *zaâfrane beldi* means that the saffron is Moroccan; *hammed roumi* means that the lemon is a larger variety and not one of the smaller, local types.

INGREDIENTS

ALMONDS

FR: *amandes*, **MOR:** *louz*

Few meals seem to lack at least a few crunchy almonds scattered over the top of a dish. The nuts remain an important crop around Tafraoute and the Ameln Valley in the southern Anti-Atlas, where the almonds tend to be smallish with a sharply pointed end.

Toasting or frying almonds deepens their taste and gives them a pleasing crunch.

To remove skins from raw almonds: Blanch in boiling water for a few seconds, drain, and immediately dunk in a basin of cold water. Drain, place on a paper towel or kitchen towel, and rub until the skins slip off.

To dry-toast: Preheat the oven to 400°F/200°C/gas mark 6. Place the almonds on an ungreased baking sheet and bake, shaking the pan from time to time, until golden and fragrant, about 10 minutes. Transfer to a plate to cool.

To fry: In a small saucepan, heat light olive oil over medium-high heat and add the almonds. Fry, stirring to cook them evenly, until golden, 1 to 2 minutes. Transfer with a slotted spoon to paper towels to drain.

ARGAN OIL

FR: *huile d'argane*, **MOR:** *zit argan*

This rich, nutty, dark golden oil is one of the country's most prized—and expensive—food products. The limited and labor-intensive production is done nowadays almost exclusively in women's co-ops.

Indigenous to the Souss region of the Anti-Atlas, thorny, sprawling argan trees produce a yellow fruit that is left to fall and shrivel in summer. From what looks something like a date, a nut is pressed out, and the shell is cracked open with a flat stone. Inside is what is referred to as an *amande* (almond). These are ground to extract the oil. To make 1 qt/1 L of argan oil, it takes roughly 220 lb/100 kg fresh fruit from the tree, 82 lb/37 kg dried fruit, 55 lb/25 kg nuts, and 5½ to 6½ lb/2.5 to 3 kg *amandes*. Nothing in the process is wasted. The shells are used to heat the *hammam* and bread ovens, and the outer fruit and pressed residue are fed to goats.

Locals drizzle argan oil onto salads and couscous, and dip bread in a bowl of the oil for breakfast or with tea for a morning or afternoon snack. It is also blended with honey and ground almonds into a thick dip for bread called *amlou*.

For argan oil, substitute walnut oil.

COUSCOUS

MOR: *kuskus*, **BERBER:** *sksou*

Couscous refers to both the dish and the tiny "grains" formed from hard durum wheat or sometimes corn. Couscous grains are steamed, uncovered, in a perforated basket over a fragrant stew until light and fluffy, mounded on a platter, and covered with the stew. Couscous comes in various types and sizes.

FRESHLY ROLLED: To make couscous from scratch, two different calibers of ground semolina, moistened with a touch of salted water, are rolled into tiny beads in a large, sloped-edged platter called a *gsâa* (see page 53). Sifted through a round sieve, or *ghorbal*, to ensure uniform size, they are left to dry. This time-consuming process is uncommon today.

STANDARD: A number of excellent brands of couscous are on the market—Tria and Dari are favorites in Morocco. The grains need to be moistened with cool water and left to sit and swell before being steamed two or three times for a total of 45 to 60 minutes. Between steamings, the grains are moistened with cool water and rested, and any clumps worked out. See page 173 for preparing couscous in this traditional manner.

QUICK COOKING: Outside North Africa, most couscous sold in supermarkets is the "quick-cooking," "instant," or "precooked" variety (in French, *précuit*). Instructions normally indicate that it takes just 5 minutes or so to prepare. Yet following the package directions usually results mushy, clumpy couscous. To maximize its potential—quick-cooking couscous can be just about as light and fluffy as the standard variety—see page 171.

NONWHEAT: Barley—*shir* in Moroccan Arabic, *timzin* or *ibrine* in Berber—was perhaps the original grain used by Berbers to make couscous, and it continues to be popular in Berber-dominated regions. Known as *belboula* in Moroccan Arabic, *sksou n'timzin* or *sksou n'ibrine* in Berber, and *couscous d'orge* in French, barley couscous is darker and earthier tasting than semolina wheat couscous, and needs three steamings. Morocco-based Dari produces an excellent quick-cooking barley couscous.

Significantly less common is a corn-based couscous called *baddaz*, a specialty of El Jadida, south of Casablanca.

SIZES: The most common size is medium (look for the French word *moyen* on packaging), followed by fine. Although some dishes might typically use a particular size, such as fine for sweet couscous, the choice nearly always comes down to personal preference.

MHAMSA or BERKOUKÈS: Akin to large grains of couscous, these are usually made, and treated, like tiny pasta pellets—added to simmering liquid—though they can also be steamed in a couscoussier. They are more popular in the north of Morocco, and among certain Berbers who drizzle them with olive oil and give them to pregnant women for energy.

DATES

FR: *dattes*, **MOR:** *tmar;* **SINGULAR:** *tamra*

Dates in Morocco are a staple as well as a symbol. They are traditionally offered to guests with a glass of milk and are the first item eaten with the breaking of the fast during Ramadan.

Moroccans eat on average more than 6 lb/2.7 kg of dates each year, though in some date-growing areas, that figure is around 33 lb/15 kg; half of that amount is consumed during the month of Ramadan. They eat dates out of hand after a meal or as a snack; munch on them for energy while working in the date regions; stuff them with almond paste for elaborate sweets, and use them to decorate sweet couscous for dessert. Innovative cooks have begun exploring the date's culinary potential, from churning them into ice cream to—in the case of one young entrepreneur in the village of Timiderte, just south of Agdz in the Drâa Valley—commercially preparing marmalade from dark *bousthammi* dates as well as a blend of lighter brown varieties.

The main date palm groves are in Ouarzazate and along the Drâa Valley, including the large El Faïja grove in Zagora; in the eastern and southern oases (Errachidia in the Ziz Valley, Erfoud, Figuig, Tata, Guelmim, and Tiznit); and around Agadir and Marrakech. Date trees blossom in spring, and harvesting begins in October. The palms of the tree are used for fuel and to make screens to block the wind, and are woven into mats, furniture, and baskets.

The wood from the trunk is carved into gutters and roof beams. Bayoud disease continues to threaten Moroccan groves, though certain varieties seem slightly less susceptible than others.

Government statistics say that Morocco has 223 varieties of dates. There are also around 1,800 hybrid varieties, which are generically called *khalts*. Following are some of the most common varieties.

AGUELLID: Golden yellow, soft, and sweet. The name is Berber and means "king." Sometimes called by the Arabic translation, *malik tmar*.

AZIZA: Golden tan and smallish. A favorite of Figuig.

BOUFEGGOUS: Sweet, semisoft variety that stores well. Found in Ouarzazate.

BOURAR: Big and brown. Found in the Drâa.

BOUSKRI: Light, olive colored, and pleasantly sweet (the name refers to sugar). They can be picked very soft, but many locals prefer to eat them drier so that the crisp skin shatters when bitten into. Bayoud disease has ravaged this variety, and fewer are harvested each year.

BOUSLIKHÈNE: Very sweet, with a thick, dried skin. A specialty of Errachidia.

BOUSTHAMMI: Dark, almost black, small (about 1¼ in/ 3 cm long), semidry and chewy, and pleasantly sweet, these are a favorite in the Drâa Valley and Zagora, where they are one of the main varieties grown.

BUETTOB: Possessing a very small pit. A specialty of Tata.

HALAWI: Smaller than *mejhoul*, these soft, wrinkled dates have a high sugar content and are a favorite to eat for dessert.

JIHEL: A filling, high-quality date from a tree that produces on alternating years. Popular in the Drâa Valley.

MAKF: Black or dark, like *bousthammi*. Found in Zagora.

MEJHOUL: The best-known Moroccan variety is the one used for ceremonies and special dishes. Dark caramel brown, soft, and wrinkled with meaty flesh, the dates are large and deeply flavorful. They account for only 0.3 percent or so of the country's total production.

DRIED FIGS
FR: *figues séchées*, MOR: *sriha*

Gritty, grainy, and sweet, dried figs come in two main varieties. The most common found in Morocco are pale yellow ones, flattened and stacked or strung together. The fatter, pear-shaped type also works in the recipes in this book. Remove the stems before using, if desired. For figs that are very dry, soak in water for a few hours before adding to a recipe. Fresh figs are called *kermus*.

DRIED APRICOTS
FR: *abricots séchées*, MOR: *meshmash yabes*

More acidic than their fresh counterparts, dried apricots are the least sweet dried fruit. They contribute an appealing tartness, brilliant color, and chewy texture to tagines, and are often coupled with prunes. To rehydrate dried apricots before using, soak them in water or orange juice or simmer in water sweetened with sugar. Fresh apricots are called *meshmash*.

HONEY
FR: *miel*, MOR: *assal*

Used to caramelize onions and fruits for tagines, found in desserts and sweets, eaten for breakfast with flatbreads, or drizzled over yogurt, honey is a key ingredient in the Moroccan pantry. It's also a base for many traditional medicines and ancient therapeutics, used internally and externally, and is lauded in the Qur'an. Honey has a symbolic role in Morocco at weddings, at births, and during mourning, when it's served for three days following a death.

The country's main apiculture areas are the Gharb region in the northwest, especially around the citrus-growing towns of Sidi Slimane and nearby Sidi Kacem, and in the Souss hills northeast of Agadir, namely around the villages of Imouzzer des Ida Outanane and Argana. Argana has one of the oldest collective beehives in the world, consisting of hundreds of boxes rising stories high, whose ownership is distributed among the villagers.

Bees gather nectar from various sources, each of which imparts a slightly different flavor to the honey. Favorites include orange blossom, thyme, lavender, and eucalyptus (especially good for the throat). The honeys range in color from pale amber to almost black.

KHLEA

These dried, seasoned strips of beef are an ancient way of preserving meat. Marinated in seasonings, such as salt, garlic, cumin, sweet paprika, and crushed coriander seeds, the strips are sun-dried, boiled, and then stored in pots of rendered fat. *Khlea* imparts its unique flavor most commonly in lentils (especially in winter), certain tagines, and eggs.

LBEN

Buttermilk, a slightly acidic drink that is a by-product of the butter-making process, is a favorite to accompany couscous. It's usually made from cow's milk, though also from the milk of sheep, goats, and, in the far south of the country, camel.

OLIVE OIL
FR: *huile d'olive*, MOR: *zit zeytun*

Until the 1960s, when corn and other vegetable oils hit the local market, olive oil was the main oil used in home kitchens. Although now accounting for around only 16 percent of the county's oil consumption, it remains an important industry. Along with the modern pressing facilities, there are some sixteen thousand traditional oil mills, called *maâsras*, in the rural growing areas. Many of these artisanal presses use a stone wheel turned by a donkey or mule and press only enough oil to be consumed locally or by the producers themselves.

OLIVES
FR: *olives*, MOR: *zeytun*

Remains of oil mills and vessels found at ancient sites show that cultivation of olives in Morocco goes back to the first millennium BCE. Phoenicians introduced the olive tree, Romans expanded cultivation, and over the centuries, techniques of irrigation and oil production were gradually perfected. Today, Morocco has three main olive-growing areas: in the northern Rif Mountains (around Chefchaouen, Taounate, and Ouazzane); in the center of the country (around Taza, Fès, and Meknès); and in the south (around Haouz, Tadla, and coastal Safi and Essaouira).

Moroccan groves produce both table olives—Morocco is the world's number-two exporter after Spain—and olives for oil. Nearly all the olives grown are the

variety Picholine Marocaine, which has a dual role of being used on the table and pressed into oil. The remaining crop consists of Picholine du Languedoc, Dahbia, and Meslala, plus the Spanish varieties Picual, Arbequina, and Gordal, and the Italian Frantoio.

Morocco is known for its dry curing—olives cured not in brine but packed under layers of salt for weeks, or even months, before being washed and lightly coated with olive oil. This process draws out most of the bitterness and gives the olives a wrinkled, prunelike appearance and chewy texture. The taste is intense and aromatic, a bit salty with a hint of smoky bitterness at the finish.

PRESERVED LEMONS
FR: *citrons confits*, MOR: *hammed masseyer*

Preserved lemons, a trademark of Moroccan cuisine, are a unique ingredient whose tight, tart flavor adds a pungent boost to dishes from salads to baked fish and chicken tagines.

Although preserved lemons are easy to find in Moroccan markets, many cooks still prepare them at home, as the process is quite simple (see facing page). Sliced open and packed with salt, the lemons are stored in glass jars and immersed in lemon juice. After a month, they soften and their flavor intensifies. The lemons keep for around 6 months. Before using them, rinse lightly with water. Some recipes use only the peel, after the pulp is scraped out and discarded. Others call for chopping the pulp and using it instead of, or along with, the peel.

For preserving lemons, use aromatic, thin-skinned lemons, such as smooth-skinned, juicy Meyers. Thicker-skinned lemons should be soaked first in water for 2 to 3 days, changing the water daily.

In Morocco, two small local varieties are favorites: *boussera*, with its distinctive nipple end, which is more typical in the spring and in the south, and the even smaller *doqq*, which comes from a tree that flowers beautifully but has a small yield of fruit. Unfortunately, *doqqs* are becoming less common in the markets. As one merchant in Fès told me, "The city was once surrounded by small gardens that grew *doqq*. But now there is too much construction and they are harder to find." The same can be said about many cities across the country. Larger, often juicier commercial lemons known as *hammed roumi* are now more common.

A comparable substitution for preserved lemon is hard to find. Using lemon juice is ineffective. Adding lemon zest at the end of cooking, though, will give a stew a hint of tangy pungency.

PRUNES

FR: *pruneaux,* **MOR:** *barqoq*

Dark, shriveled, and sticky dried plums are even sweeter than the fresh version. Use prunes with pits in tagines and braised dishes, as they retain their shape and texture better during cooking.

RAISINS

FR: *raisins secs,* **MOR:** *zbib*

Sweet, dried grapes are integral to many sweet-and-savory combinations, and dark or golden raisins are in countless dishes, from vegetable couscouses to desserts. Unless you are adding the raisins to a long-simmering tagine or couscous sauce, soak them in warm water for 10 minutes and drain before using.

SEMOLINA

FR: *semoule,* **MOR:** *smida*

Ground hard durum wheat comes in two sizes, fine and coarse. Both are used to hand-roll couscous from scratch. Fine semolina can be found in certain breads, cookies, and desserts, and as a base for a type of soup.

SMEN

Clarified and preserved salted butter gives a distinctive earthy—some would say cheesy or almost dank—flavor and aroma to a number of traditional dishes. Rubbed into couscous and over spit-roasting lamb (*mechoui*), used to cook onions (as in the beloved chicken in *khdra* sauce with almonds), and added to white beans, lentils, *harira* soup, or *tangia* stew, it draws out savory flavors and adds depth.

Smen falls somewhere between *zebda* (fresh, but slightly pungent farm or country butter) and *boudra* (rancid butter used rarely in the kitchen and more

PRESERVED LEMONS

MAKES 6 TO 8 PRESERVED LEMONS

About 10 thin-skinned lemons
Coarse sea salt

Sterilize a 1-qt/1-L glass canning jar in a boiling water bath.

Scrub the lemons well. Remove any wax by dunking the lemons into boiling water and firmly wiping off the wax.

Coat the bottom of the jar with salt.

Working over a bowl to catch any juice, cut each lemon lengthwise into quarters, leaving the quarters attached at the stem end. Gently open the lemon and pack with salt, then coat the outside with salt. Place a lemon right-side up in the jar and press down on it with a wooden spoon to release some juice. Repeat the process, placing each lemon snugly beside or on top of another and pushing down with the spoon to release some juice. Depending on the size of the lemons and the shape of the jar, you should fit 6 to 8 of the lemons. Add any accumulated juice from the bowl.

The lemons need to be completely covered with juice. Squeeze the remaining lemons as needed into the jar to cover the lemons completely. Invert the jar two or three times to mix. Keep the jar in a dark, cool place, turning it from time to time during the first week. The lemons will be ready to use after 1 month. Remove from the jar with a clean wooden spoon. Add lemon juice as needed to keep the lemons covered.

commonly for massage and aromatherapy). These days *smen* is rarely made at home, as it is easy to buy in Morocco.

Always remove *smen* with a dry spoon to prevent bacteria from forming in the jar. Substitute with regular salted butter or, if desired, for a hint of the cheesiness, a small crumbled piece of blue cheese.

VERMICELLI
FR: *vermicelle*, **MOR:** *shariya*

These short, thin noodles are added to soups, and even steamed in a couscoussier, sweetened, and eaten on their own or as a side dish. About 1 in/2.5 cm long, they come in different thicknesses: fine for sweet pasta; thicker for *harira* soup and for adding to warm milk for a simple evening meal. Substitute spaghettini, capellini, or angel hair pasta broken into 1-in/2.5-cm lengths. The word comes from the Moroccan Arabic for "hair," *shar*.

WALNUTS
FR: *noix*, **MOR:** *gergaâ*

Commonly found in desserts, walnuts grow most notably east of Marrakech on the slopes of the Atlas Mountains in the Ourika Valley and around Midelt on the southern side of the Middle Atlas. The wood of the tree makes the finest wide, shallow platters, or *gsâa*, used for preparing couscous and dough (see page 53).

WARQA (or OUARKA)

The fine, paper-thin pastry sheets used for savory stuffed pastries and layered desserts are made by smearing a fine coating of damp, sticky, elastic dough across a wide, hot griddle before peeling it off after 15 seconds or so in a single, fluid motion. *Warqa* is famously difficult to make, and most Moroccans buy fresh sheets in the market or commercial brands in stores.

Sheets of phyllo (also called filo) pastry, though slightly thicker, are an excellent substitution, as are Chinese spring roll wrappers. Two common sizes of phyllo sheets are 12 by 17 in/30.5 by 43 cm and 9 by 14 in/23 by 35.5 cm.

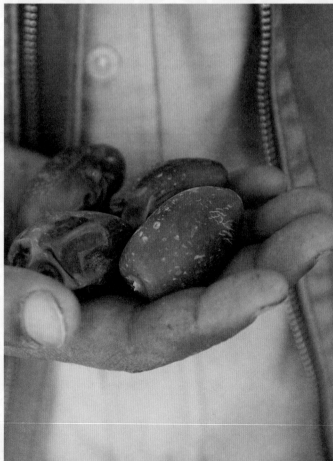

THE COMPLETE MOROCCAN SPICE BOX

The ample Moroccan spice box includes such essentials as black pepper, cinnamon, ginger, cumin, saffron, turmeric, sweet paprika, and dried hot red pepper. For fresh herbs, the most important are cilantro (coriander) and flat-leaf parsley, and for dried, a local oregano called *zaâtar*.

Moroccans have mastered the art of blending spices not only in individual dishes—say, a sweet tagine with cinnamon, ginger, nutmeg, turmeric, and saffron—but also in spice blends containing dozens of ingredients. The most famous is *ras el hanout* (page 52). A number of spices rarely used on their own are found only in this heady blend.

Spices begin to lose their potency once they are ground, so it's preferable to grind them at home as needed, or to buy small, freshly ground amounts in the *attarine* (spice *souq*) from a trusted *attar* (spice merchant). To grind spices, use a mortar and pestle, spice grinder, or clean coffee grinder. Store the spices in a dry, dark, cool place.

AROMATIC HERBS

ABSINTHE (FR: *absinthe*, MOR: *shiba*): Sprigs of this pale, silvery plant, with delicate, fine leaves that hint of anise, are added to mint tea in winter to reinforce the flavor and add a bit of warmth. Add the leaves at the end of the preparation and infuse for 30 seconds to 1 minute, as the flavor quickly becomes bitter. Some northern Moroccans also combine absinthe with dried rosebuds for a cold-weather infusion. Also called absinthe wormwood or wormwood.

BASIL (FR: *basilic*, MOR: *lahbaq*): Although the most common use for this strong-smelling, bright green herb is as a potted plant to ward off mosquitoes, some Atlas Berbers use it in salads.

BAY LEAF (FR: *laurier*, MOR: *wraq sidna mûsa*): A robust herb with strong, warm tones. The dried leaves tend to be slightly less bitter than fresh ones, though they are also used. Bruising fresh leaves brings out sweet notes. To bruise, hold both ends of the leaf and twist in opposite directions.

CILANTRO (FR: *coriandre*, MOR: *qesbur*): Supple and slightly pungent, cilantro—also called fresh coriander—is one of Morocco's most distinct flavorings. Cooks frequently pair it with parsley, and chop both the parsleylike leaves and the stems. Store with a damp paper towel wrapped around the stems or stand the bunch upright in a jar of water.

FENNEL (FR: *fenouil*, MOR: *ennafaâ*): The fennel bulb and its feathery leaves are used to infuse some soups and fish dishes with their lovely anise notes, including fish on the grill. Dried stalks can also be tucked inside grilled fish. See page 49 for fennel seeds.

GARLIC (FR: *ail*, MOR: *touma*): A favorite in the Moroccan kitchen, garlic is used more frequently in winter than in summer, and is generally preferred cooked as opposed to raw. Moroccan garlic heads are small, pink, and fragrant. Look for compact heads, heavy for their size, and avoid yellowish or overly dry ones. Remove any green sprouts from the center. Store in a cool, dry place.

LAVENDER (FR: *lavande*, MOR: *khzama*): Rarely used on their own, dried tiny purple lavender flowers give a floral sweetness to *ras el hanout* and, on occasion, to tea. Grown in the Middle Atlas.

LEMON VERBENA (FR: *verveine citronnelle*, MOR: *louiza*): Sold in large burlap bags across the country (and especially popular in the north), dried verbena is used in tea or as an infusion. It's an excellent digestive and is well known for its calming properties. Infused in milk, it makes a relaxing evening drink. The plant is cultivated across Morocco, especially where it receives abundant sun and can be protected from strong winds.

MARJORAM (FR: *marjolaine*, MOR: *mardaddûch*): A leafy green herb that is closely related to oregano and carries a similar, if slightly sweeter, flavor. It's a key ingredient in the bouillon for snails sold at street stalls and is sometimes added to tea with other fresh herbs in winter.

MINT (FR: *menthe verte*, MOR: *naânaâ*): Thanks to ubiquitous glasses of tea made with fresh mint, this is undoubtedly the herb most associated with Morocco. There are two kinds: peppermint—used mostly in

medicine and as breath fresheners—and spearmint. Cooks prefer the narrow, brilliant green leaves of fresh Moroccan spearmint, which is sold and used in great quantities across the country.

OREGANO (FR: *origan*, MOR: *zaâtar*): Crumbled dried oregano brings a sharp, savory flavor to many dishes. The extremely popular Moroccan variety is called *zaâtar* (see below).

PARSLEY (FR: *persil*, MOR: *madnus*): Moroccans use a good deal of fresh flat-leaf parsley (sometimes called Italian, as opposed to curly), often coupled with fresh cilantro. Store with a damp paper towel wrapped around the stems or stand the bunch upright in a jar of water.

SAGE (FR: *sauge*, MOR: *salmya*): Fresh, velvety, silvery green leaves of sage fortify pots of winter tea or are used alone for an herbal infusion.

THYME (FR: *thym*, MOR: *azzâitra*): This hearty shrub, with gray-green leaves and small-budded white flowers, is usually used in dried form. It is less popular than its cousins, oregano and *zaâtar*.

ZAÂTAR: In the Middle East, *zaâtar* is a spice blend, but in Morocco, it's a shrubby herb from the thyme and oregano family with slender leaves and clusters of purple flowers. Used in dried form, the tiny, flaky green leaves have a flavor more redolent of oregano than thyme. The best Moroccan *zaâtar* comes from the High Atlas. Substitute oregano or oregano with a pinch of thyme.

SPICES

ANISEED (FR: *graines d'anis vert*, MOR: *habbet hlawa*): These fine, ribbed seeds, ranging from tan to light green, have a warm, fruity aroma slightly more subtle than fennel seeds. They are used in breads, biscuits, and milk drinks, as well as to season chicken dishes and snails. The seeds are commonly confused with fennel seeds (*ennafaâ*) since they look so similar.

BLACK PEPPER (FR: *poivre noire*, MOR: *ibzar*): See pepper.

CARAWAY (FR: *carvi*, MOR: *karwia*): Crescent-shaped and ribbed, caraway seeds hint of anise with an added pungent nuttiness. Unground seeds flavor certain breads and soups and the broth for snails.

CARDAMOM (**FR**: *cardamome*, **MOR**: *qaâqûlla*): The plump, ribbed, green oval pods each hold fifteen to twenty tiny, dark seeds. The pods are first lightly crushed to release their pungent, bittersweet warmth. When buying cardamom, look for pods that are yellowish green, as opposed to pale.

CAYENNE PEPPER (**FR**: *piment fort*, **MOR**: *felfla soudaniya* or *soudaniya*): Very hot red pepper found commonly in the south, where influences from West Africa came up through the desert on ancient caravans. Cayenne is similar to chili powder (*felfla harra*), though it is from a different, southern source.

CHASTE TREE BERRIES (**FR**: *poivre des moines*, **MOR**: *kheroua*): The fruit of the chaste tree. This aromatic, slightly bitter spice most often appears in *ras el hanout*. Also called monk's pepper.

CHILI POWDER (**FR**: *piment piquant*, **MOR**: *felfla harra*): See cayenne pepper.

CINNAMON (**FR**: *canelle*, **MOR**: *qarfa*): Hot and sharp with a sweet aftertaste, cinnamon is used in both sweet and savory dishes. Cinnamon is sold ground and in pieces of bark. The latter have a more pronounced flavor than quills, which are less common in Morocco. There are two kinds of cinnamon, true cinnamon and cassia. Though the former is technically called *dar sini*, locals nearly always refer to both as *qarfa*.

CLOVE (**FR**: *clou de girofle*, **MOR**: *oud annawar*): This dried, unopened flower bud has a warm, peppery sweetness. Used in both sweet and savory dishes, and found in *ras el hanout*.

CORIANDER SEEDS (**FR**: *graines de coriandre*, **MOR**: *qesbur yabes*): Although fresh coriander (known also as cilantro; see page 47) is far more common in Morocco, some cooks add the crushed seeds to dishes such as ground *kefta*, chicken tagines, and occasionally lamb. Hinting of anise, with a pungent lemoniness, the round, pale brown seeds exude a slight, lingering sweetness. To deepen the flavor of the seeds before grinding them, toast in a small, dry skillet for 1 to 3 minutes until aromatic.

CUBEB PEPPER (**FR**: *cubèbe*, **MOR**: *kabbaba*): Also known as tailed pepper or Java pepper, cubeb resembles a black peppercorn with a little stalk or tail protruding from one end. Cubeb adds a fresh pepperiness and hint of pine to *ras el hanout*.

CUMIN (**FR**: *cumin*, **MOR**: *kamûne*): The distinct taste of cumin—warm and earthy, slightly bitter, with aromas of hay—is one of the defining flavors of savory Moroccan cooking. The slightly curved and ridged brown seeds are used in ground form and are added to an array of dishes, from cooked salads and soups to skewers of grilled fish and chicken. In the south, where the best cumin is produced, a dish of the ground spice often sits on the table beside salt and black pepper.

FENNEL SEEDS (**FR**: *graines de fenouil*, **MOR**: *ennafaâ*): These light brown, slightly curved seeds have a subtle anise aroma and a lightly bittersweet aftertaste. The name is commonly confused with aniseed (*habbet hlawa*).

FENUGREEK (**FR**: *fenugrec*, **MOR**: *halba*): These dark seeds need to be toasted to release their burnt sugary taste. Be careful not to dry-toast them too long, or the bitterness becomes pronounced.

GALANGA ROOT (**FR**: *galanga*, **MOR**: *khûdanjal*): This knobby, pale root of the ginger family is infused in certain teas for its peppery ginger tones. It's an important ingredient in *atay melouki* (King Tea), a popular hot drink in Marrakech's Djemaa el Fna square. Galanga is sometimes added to *ras el hanout*.

GINGER (**FR**: *gingembre*, **MOR**: *skinjbir*): Usually used in dried, ground form, ginger adds a hot sweetness to savory dishes and a note of spice to sweet ones. Frequently combined with cinnamon and sometimes nutmeg. The sharp flavor mellows with cooking.

GRAINS OF PARADISE (**FR**: *maniguette*, **MOR**: *guza sahrawiya*): This cousin of cardamom from the ginger and artichoke family has an egg-size seedpod with sixty to one hundred small, dark, and peppery-hot seeds. Hard to find outside of West and North Africa, it was carried to Morocco and Europe on the ancient Saharan caravans. Found almost exclusively in *ras el hanout*. Also called Guinea pepper or melegueta pepper.

GUM ARABIC or **GUM ACACIA** (**FR:** *gomme arabique,* **MOR:** *meska horra* or *aâlk*): The hardened sap from a species of wild acacia tree found on the arid savannahs that rim the southern edge of the Sahara. The translucent, crystal-like pieces range from pale to red. Gum arabic acts as a natural binding agent, giving consistent texture to pastries, some sweet dishes, and teas and coffees. Crush pieces with a pinch of sugar to keep them from sticking to the mortar. Rather flavorless and odorless, gum arabic is similar to mastic (see below) but without the piney notes. Outside Morocco, good spice shops should have, or be able to get, gum arabic.

JUNIPER BERRIES (**FR:** *baies de genièvre,* **MOR:** *arar*): Bluish black berries with a piney, spicy freshness. They are used both fresh and dried. Found largely in *ras el hanout.*

LICORICE (**FR:** *réglisse,* **MOR:** *âarq sûs*): A shrub with bright yellow wood, licorice has a sweet and warm aniselike flavor. It's a key ingredient in the snails sold from street stalls, as well as a favorite for kids to chew on. Use pencil-sized pieces of root, as opposed to extracted forms that have been molded into hard, shiny black shapes or ground as powder.

LONG PEPPER (**FR:** *poivre long,* **MOR:** *dhar elfelfel*): Dried and ground, the finger-shaped rods have a similar taste to peppercorns, though they are hotter, more pungent, and slightly musky. Found in *ras el hanout.* Sometimes called *pippali.*

MACE (**FR:** *macis,* **MOR:** *bsibisa*): Dried and ground, the lacy red netlike covering of a nutmeg kernel has a similar, although softer flavor than nutmeg. Substitute with one-fourth the amount of much more potent ground nutmeg.

MASTIC (**FR:** *mastic,* **MOR:** *meska horra*): The piney-flavored, slightly bitter resin or sap of a tree from the Greek island of Chios that hardens into a pale yellow to deep amber color. It's similar to gum arabic and in Morocco is called as such (see above).

NIGELLA SEEDS (**FR:** *nigelle,* **MOR:** *sanûj*): Small black seeds, earthy and mild, with peppery notes, found on occasion in bread and tagines. Dry-toast the seeds first to bring out their aroma and nutty flavor. Sometimes called black cumin or onion seeds.

NUTMEG (**FR:** *muscade,* **MOR:** *gouza et tib*): Potently sweet and spicy, nutmeg comes ground, but buying the whole spherical kernel and grating it fresh is the best way to preserve its aroma.

ORRIS ROOT (**FR:** *iris,* **MOR:** *oud ambar*): Ground powder from the root of a Florentine iris that adds a floral note to *ras el hanout.* Grown in the High Atlas.

PEPPER: The tiny berries are harvested at different stages, with each type of dried peppercorn—black, white, red or pink, green—offering distinct characteristics. Black, which is aromatic, pungent, warm, and hinting of citrus, is the most common. Creamy-colored white peppercorns are less aromatic but often preferred in lighter-colored dishes. Red or pink peppercorns have almost a berry flavor to their softer spiciness. Green peppercorns tend to be fresher and hotter.

ROSEBUDS (**FR:** *boutons de roses,* **MOR:** *ward*): With strong peppery, floral flavors and musky aromas, rosebuds are rarely used alone and are most commonly found in *ras el hanout.* Occasionally, during the damp cold winters of northern Morocco, they are infused with fresh absinthe leaves for a hot drink. The rose's most common culinary use in Morocco is as the aromatic distillation rose water (see page 52).

SAFFRON (**FR:** *safran,* **MOR:** *az zaâfrane al hûrr* or *zaâfrane*): Perhaps brought to Morocco's shores thousands of years ago by Phoenician traders, saffron grows on the dry Anti-Atlas Souktana plateau between 4,000 and 5,000 ft/1,200 and 1,520 m. The extreme conditions—brutally hot summers, bitter cold winters—give strength to the color and pungency to the aroma. Taliouine, in the province of Taroudant, between Ouarzazate and Agadir, is Morocco's undisputed saffron capital.

Cultivating and collecting the world's most expensive spice is a delicate and laborious process. Each small, violet-petaled flower has just three red-orange stigmas; it takes some 70,000 flowers to yield 1 lb/450 g of saffron. The harvest lasts over a four- to six-week period in autumn and peaks at the end of October, when about 60 percent of the flowers

bloom together during a two-week window. During this time, whole families work together to gather flowers and then remove the precious stigmas.

When buying saffron, look for deep red to purple threads. Avoid the powder, which might be adulterated or at least will lose its flavor faster. Store saffron away from light, which damages flavor.

To reap saffron's full potential, dry-toast the threads in a small skillet for 1 to 2 minutes over medium heat. Then crush the threads with the back of a spoon in a bowl or with a pestle in a mortar. Alternatively, fold a clean sheet of paper in half, place the toasted threads inside, fold over the paper, and crush between the fingers; open and shake into the dish.

One pinch of saffron equals about twenty threads.

SESAME SEEDS (FR: *graines de sésame,* **MOR:** *janjlane*): A sprinkling of toasted sesame seeds over stewed fruits (both fresh and dried) in a tagine adds a welcome texture, taste, and decorative element. The seeds are used frequently to garnish breads, biscuits, and cookies, and are often added to spiced coffee blends.

To dry-toast sesame seeds, heat a small, dry skillet over medium-low heat. Sprinkle in the seeds and shake until they are golden and aromatic and they begin to jump around the pan.

SWEET PAPRIKA (FR: *piment rouge doux,* **MOR:** *felfla hloua* or *tahmira*): Sweet ground red pepper finds its way into numerous dishes for both its flavor and its natural coloring. Substitute unsmoked Spanish *pimentón dulce.*

TURMERIC (FR: *curcuma,* **MOR:** *al kharqûm*): Dried turmeric roots are ground into a bright, mustard yellow spice, which not only naturally colors a dish but adds a slight woody, gingery flavor. Significantly less expensive than saffron, ground turmeric is often used as a substitute, though both the taste and the finish are coarser.

WHITE PEPPER (FR: *poivre blanc,* **MOR:** *ibzar abiad*): See pepper.

SPICE BLENDS

HARISSA: This spicy chile paste is originally from Tunisia, where dried hot peppers from the Cap Bon peninsula are blended with garlic, olive oil, and spices such as coriander and caraway. *Harissa* has found its way onto many Moroccan tables. Some local versions include preserved lemon, giving the heat a pleasing tartness and distinctive Moroccan stamp. Stir a dollop into couscous broth for extra punch.

MSAKHEN: This traditional spice blend in the south has a wide variety of ingredients, although generally fewer than *ras el hanout*. *Msakhen* is considered medicinal—as an aphrodisiac and aid to conception—and is also used as a spice for food. The same Marrakech *attar* who recommended the *ras el hanout* below includes two dozen ingredients in *msakhen*, among them wild mint, watercress, pomegranate flowers, mace, lavender, thyme, and grains of paradise. Add a pinch to fried eggs or a chicken tagine.

RAS EL HANOUT: Aromatic, hot, and sensual, this is Morocco's iconic spice blend. The name translates to "head [or top] of shop" and can include fifty different spices, or as few as twenty. Although the composition changes by region and the discretion of the spice merchant (*attar*), certain spices are almost always present—ginger, cardamom, mace, cubeb pepper, black pepper, and turmeric, and, for floral notes, rosebud and lavender. The Indian spice blend garam masala is a good substitution, though it is often hotter, so reduce the amount slightly.

Ras el hanout is commercially available, but a simplified, bare-bones version, using a minimum of ingredients, can be prepared at home. This comes from an *attar* that I trust in Marrakech when I asked him to design a blend using twelve spices. Missing are some of the usual components in a more complete blend, but the balance is right. He combined fenugreek, cinnamon, turmeric, ginger, coriander seeds, white pepper, long pepper, nutmeg, a local wild cumin (known as *kamûne es sûfi*; substitute caraway), sesame seeds, rosemary, and saffron. Quantities of each vary greatly depending if you want a sweeter or hotter version, though either way use nutmeg and saffron sparingly. For a milder mix, replace the white pepper with star anise or licorice, and for added aroma, include some dried rosebuds or lavender.

AROMATICS

ORANGE FLOWER WATER (**FR:** *eau de fleur d'oranger*, **MOR:** *ma zhar*): Distilled from an infusion of bitter orange blossoms, this *aromate* dazzles salads and desserts, glasses of milk, tagines, and, on special occasions, bread. Use in moderation if you are unaccustomed to its potentially overpowering flavor. Also called orange blossom water.

ROSE WATER (**FR:** *eau de rose*, **MOR:** *ma ward*): Distilled from the petals of pink roses—*rosa damascena*, known in Morocco as *al ward al baldi*. Perhaps carried to Morocco as far back as 1100 CE by pilgrims returning from Mecca, the roses have been cultivated for many centuries in the "Valley of the Roses" on the sun-baked eastern slopes of the High Atlas. The distinctive, sometimes defining aroma of rose water finds its way into countless sweet dishes and pastries. Use in moderation if you are unaccustomed to its potentially overpowering flavor.

KEY MOROCCAN KITCHEN TOOLS

Foremost among the handful of special tools in the Moroccan kitchen are the tagine and the couscoussier. While in rural areas some still cook tagines on charcoal braziers, every kitchen today has a well-used pressure cooker (or two) and usually a microwave. I have not included some of the traditional tools of interest only to the specialist, such as the *ghorbal* (a sieve made of pierced leather or wire mesh for sifting couscous grains), *chtato* (a silk-lined sieve for sifting flour), and *tbiqa* (a conical wicker basket often decorated with colorful yarn for storing bread).

CHARCOAL BRAZIER

MOR: *majmar*

There are two main versions of cooking braziers that sit on the floor. Round, unglazed ceramic braziers are used for cooking tagines. They generally stand about 7 in/17 cm high. The bowl-like top that holds the charcoal measure is about 12 in/30.5 cm across. The tagine rests on three top prongs. Small round Weber barbecues make adequate substitutions. Rectangular, usually tin braziers are used for grilling fish and brochettes. Use a small barbecue or hibachi grill instead.

COUSCOUSSIER

MOR: *gedra wa al kiskes*

This two-level pot—in English most often spelled the French way, *couscoussier*—is used for both cooking the stew and steaming the couscous grains. The stew goes in the potbellied bottom section (*gedra*) and the grains in the perforated top section (*kiskes*) that fits tightly over it. As the brothy stew simmers, the steam cooks the grains above while bestowing them with flavor.

Though once terra-cotta, couscoussiers these days are nearly always metal—sturdy stainless steel, or even copper, though most are made from lighter, cheaper aluminum.

SEALING A COUSCOUSSIER: The two sections of a couscoussier need to have a good seal between them so that the steam forces itself up through the grains. Traditionally, cooks painted a band of flour and water around the joint. But this is messy, impractical, and rarely done any longer. A simpler and cleaner

method is to lay a strip of aluminum foil or plastic wrap around the rim of the bottom of the couscoussier and press the top snugly over it.

SUBSTITUTING: A large pot with a colander or steamer basket fitted over the top works well as an alternative. The pot needs to have plenty of space for the liquid below, as well as a good seal between the pot and the basket to keep the steam from escaping.

GSÂA

This wide, shallow platter with slightly sloped sides, used for preparing couscous and mixing and kneading dough, is basically a portable workspace. In the north and around Fès, the platters tend to be terra-cotta. The best are made from the wood of the walnut tree (in French, *bois de noyer*) from the Ourika Valley on the western slope of the High Atlas, and sometimes from oak (*bois de chêne*).

Standard sizes range from 16 to 20 in/40.5 to 51 cm in diameter, though larger ones are not uncommon. Crafted from a single piece of wood, they are heavy, around 1½ in/4 cm thick, and very sturdy. Place a folded kitchen towel underneath the *gsâa* while working to keep it stable; dampen the towel to keep the *gsâa* from slipping when vigorously kneading bread.

MORTAR AND PESTLE

MOR: *mehraz* AND *yad mehraz*

Typically made of brass, the mortar has a heavy, sturdy base. The pestle is long and knobby. Use a smaller mortar for pounding spices such as saffron and gum arabic, and a larger one for pounding cilantro, parsley, and garlic or for crushing nuts.

PRESSURE COOKER

One of the most common pots in the modern Moroccan kitchen, the pressure cooker reduces cooking time significantly and is especially useful for dishes with long-cooking legumes, such as chickpeas, and large pieces of meat on the bone. Frequently, tagines, soups, and stews are prepared in a pressure cooker and then transferred to a tagine for a final reheating before the meal or for serving. In Morocco, the pressure cooker is called by its French name, *cocotte*

minute, or is shortened to *cocotte*, "pot." Although pressure cookers can be used in many recipes here, I have written the recipes for a standard stove top.

SKEWERS

MOR: *m'ghazel*

Skewers for brochettes are generally metal. Substitute with wooden ones; soak in water for 30 minutes or so before using to avoid burning.

TAGINE (or TAJINE)

Tagine is the name of the dish as well as the round, shallow-based terra-cotta (clay or ceramic) casserole with a tall, pointed, conical lid. The lid fits into the base's grooved rim and acts as a closed chimney. The steam rises and condenses on the wall of the lid, and the moisture falls back onto the simmering food, preventing the loss of moisture or flavor. Tagines are perfect for slow cooking, whether over an ember-filled brazier or the low to medium heat on a stove.

SIZES: Tagines generally range from 8 in/20 cm in diameter to 16 in/40.5 cm. The former serves one or two, the latter eight to ten. The most practical and common size is 10 to 12½ in/25 to 32 cm, serving four to six. Use a tagine of approximately this common size for the recipes in this book.

GLAZING: Tagines come both unglazed and glazed. Unglazed tagines tend to be "earthier" and darken deeply over time with use. Glazed tagines are especially recommended for those who cook with them infrequently, as they store better between longer gaps of use. There are also "serving tagines," which are lighter and usually decoratively patterned. They are not heat resistant, however, and are not safe to cook in.

REGIONAL VARIATIONS: *Tagra* is a popular unglazed tagine with small clay handles from the Rif Mountains; it normally does not have a lid. These tagines also come in an oval shape, ideal for cooking whole fish. From the rich soil around the Oud Laou River, between the Rif Mountains and the Mediterranean, comes a tagine with a deeper base. And a Berber tagine referred to as *chalhaoui* has a more rounded, dome-shaped lid, as opposed to a conical one.

BUYING A TAGINE: Stacks of tagines in Morocco *souqs* make a good, if heavy, purchase. Examine them carefully for cracks and chips. A number of international companies produce traditional terra-cotta vessels or significantly heavier cast-iron ones, which are excellent conductors of heat for slow cooking.

Emile Henry Flame-Top glazed terra-cotta tagines are made with a natural, high-quality clay and can be used on direct flames, on electric elements, and in the oven. They are scratch resistant and dishwasher safe. Made in France. Three sizes: 10 in/25 cm, 11 in/28 cm, and 12½ in/32 cm.

American company Le Souk's tagines are handmade in Nabeul, Tunisia. Be sure to look for the "Cookable Tagines" made from refractory clay, as the company also produces hand-painted and hand-glazed serving tagines that are not suitable for cooking. Two sizes: 9 in/23 cm and 12 in/30.5 cm.

Clay tagines from Bram, a small clayware shop in Sonoma, California, are made by potters in Egypt. Three sizes: 11 in/28 cm, 12½ in/32 cm, and 13 in/33 cm.

For tagines with cast-iron bases, Le Creuset's version has a matte enamel surface and stoneware conical top, and can be used on the stove top or in the oven. Made in France. One size: 10¾ in/27 cm.

Staub produces tagines with cast-iron bases and ceramic tops. Made in France. Two sizes: 7⅞ in/20 cm and 11 in/28 cm.

SEASONING A TAGINE: Before using for the first time, a tagine needs to be seasoned or cured to strengthen the vessel and, if it is unglazed, to remove the raw clay flavor.

To season a tagine, submerge the base and lid in water for at least 2 hours (overnight if unglazed). Remove and let dry completely. Brush the inside of the base and lid with olive oil. For an unglazed tagine, paint the entire vessel with oil. Place in a cold oven and turn on to 350°F/180°C/gas mark 4. Bake for 2 hours. Turn off the heat and allow the tagine to slowly, and completely, cool. Season the tagine again if it goes unused for a number of months.

COOKING WITH A TAGINE: Tagines should not be used over heat higher than medium on the stove or higher than 350°F/180°C/gas mark 4 in the oven. Traditionally, they are placed over a round charcoal brazier (*majmar*; see page 53). For many stovetops, it is preferable to use a metal diffuser (see below) to ensure even cooking.

The lid is rarely completely sealed closed during cooking, but is left slightly ajar to allow for some evaporation. If necessary, you can prop the lid open with the end of a wooden spoon.

DIFFUSER: A piece of thick, round metal, placed between the heat source and the terra-cotta tagine, distributes the heat for even cooking and helps to prolong the life span of the tagine.

CARE: Wash a tagine with mild soap after use. Do not let it sit in soapy water or clean it in a dishwasher. To prevent a tagine from cracking, do not place a hot tagine on a cold surface, such as marble, or refrigerate a tagine containing food and then set it directly over heat.

SUBSTITUTING: Use a heavy, flameproof casserole, a Dutch oven, or a large, heavy sauté pan or skillet. Braiser pans also work well.

TANGIA (or TANJIA)

This tall, two-handled earthen jug is used to slow-cook an eponymous stew, one of Marrakech's most famous dishes. A *tangia* needs to be cured before use, following the same process as for a tagine (see "SEASONING A TAGINE," left). Substitute with a Dutch oven, a deep casserole with a tight-fitting lid, a heavy pot, or a bean pot.

TEAPOT
MOR: *berrad*

Moroccan tea is prepared in, and served from, a spouted teapot. Teapots range from plain aluminum or enameled metal to etched stainless steel with small "feet." Tea glasses tend to be tiny and ornately decorated.

BREAD
AND
SAVORY PASTRIES

Phyllo Rolls Stuffed with Milky Rice
• 59 •

Phyllo Triangles Stuffed
with Fresh Cheese
briouats bil jben
• 61 •

Seafood Pastilla
• 62 •

Layered Berber Flatbread
rghayif
• 64 •

Black Olive, Walnut, and Onion Bread
• 66 •

Classic Round Bread
khobz
• 68 •

Bread is the cornerstone of the Moroccan diet, eaten with every meal—from the first of the day to the last—and often in between. What greater midmorning pleasure is there than a hunk of warm bread with a bowl of olives and a glass of piping-hot mint tea? Bakeries abound, as do carts selling tall stacks of round loaves, but many people continue to prepare their own bread at home, often baking the loaves in communal ovens. Walk through the medina in any city and you still see young girls carrying wooden boards holding two round flat loaves covered with a cotton kitchen cloth heading to—or from—the neighborhood oven.

The center of a classic disk-shaped loaf is soft enough to absorb the sauce from a tagine or bowl of beans, say, while the light crust is firm enough not to collapse when taking a morsel from the pan and carrying it to the mouth as the bread becomes a utensil.

Breads vary around the country, from these basic round loaves called *khobz* (see page 68) to denser ones with a blend of flours to French-style baguettes and Berber flatbreads baked in outdoor ovens. In Ouarzazate and around the Anti-Atlas, the delicious, wide, and somewhat chewy flatbread called *tafranout* is baked on a bed of hot, small, reddish purple river stones, giving the bread a distinctive patterned bottom.

For celebrations and feasts, bread is sometimes transformed from the everyday into the special. That might be as simple as adding sesame seeds and orange flower water to the dough of *khobz*, or something more elaborate, such as bread with black olives, crushed walnuts, and sautéed onions (see page 66).

Morocco also has an important tradition of savory pastries. Paper-thin sheets of pastry folded into triangles or cigar-shaped rolls around a dollop of filling are called *briouats*. The filling might be spiced ground meat or chicken, fresh cheese (see page 61), spinach, or even sweet milky rice (see facing page). Larger, round versions called *pastillas* are most famously filled with a rich chicken or pigeon mixture, though these days commonly made with seafood and thin Asian rice noodles (see page 62).

What a delicious surprise to bite into one of these small stuffed pastry appetizers and find it packed with sweet, milky rice! If desired, prepare these *briouats* in triangles, following the rolling instructions for Phyllo Triangles Stuffed with Fresh Cheese (page 61). See note for preparing the oven.

PHYLLO ROLLS
STUFFED WITH MILKY RICE

MAKES ABOUT 20 STUFFED ROLLS

½ cup/100 g short- or medium-grain rice
¾ cup/175 ml milk, plus more if needed
1 Tbsp granulated sugar
1 tsp orange flower water
1 small cinnamon stick
Salt
5 sheets phyllo dough or *warqa* (see page 46), plus more in case of breakage
Olive oil for brushing
1 egg yolk, whisked
Light olive oil or vegetable oil for frying
Powdered sugar for dusting
Ground cinnamon for dusting

In a saucepan, bring 4 cups/1 L water to a rolling boil over high heat. Add the rice, stir, and boil until the rice is about half cooked and still very al dente, about 10 minutes. Drain in a strainer but do not rinse. Immediately return the rice to the saucepan, and stir in the milk, granulated sugar, and orange flower water. Add the cinnamon stick and a pinch of salt. Bring to a boil, reduce the heat, and simmer, stirring frequently, until the rice is tender and creamy, but not mushy, and the milk is absorbed, about 10 minutes. Stir in 1 or 2 Tbsp more milk if necessary. Spoon into a wide bowl to cool. Discard the cinnamon stick.

On a clean, flat work surface, unroll the phyllo sheets. Cut into strips about 4 in/10 cm

wide and at least 9 in/23 cm long. Arrange a couple of the strips facing away from you; cover the remaining strips with plastic wrap to keep from drying out. Lightly brush the strips with olive oil.

Place 1 Tbsp of the rice centered on the end of each strip closest to you. Roll like a cigar; halfway through rolling, fold in the sides about ½ in/12 mm, and continue rolling nearly to the end. Brush the last ½ in/12 mm of the strip with the egg yolk and roll to the end. Place the rolls on a plate without letting them touch. Repeat with the remaining phyllo strips and rice.

In a medium skillet or sauté pan over high heat, heat at least ½ in/12 mm of oil until the surface shimmers. Reduce the heat to medium. Working in small batches, gently place the phyllo rolls in the oil and fry, turning once, until golden brown, 30 seconds to 1 minute. Transfer with a slotted spoon to paper towels to drain.

Stack two or three rolls on each of six plates. Dust with powdered sugar and cinnamon just before serving.

NOTE: *To bake in the oven, preheat the oven to 350°F/180°C/gas mark 4. Line a baking sheet with parchment paper, place the rolls on the paper, and brush with olive oil. Bake until golden, about 15 minutes.*

Hot, stuffed phyllo shapes called *briouats* are delectable appetizers. Folded into small triangles, cigar-shaped cylinders, or even rectangles, they come with an array of fillings, from spiced ground kefta to sweet milky rice (see page 59). My favorite is this one with fresh unsalted cheese called *jben*—especially with a brushing of honey to give the crispy rolls a pleasing sweetness. Alternatively, dust the fried *briouats* with powdered sugar and cinnamon.

PHYLLO TRIANGLES
STUFFED WITH
FRESH CHEESE

briouats bil jben

MAKES ABOUT 16 STUFFED TRIANGLES

½ lb/225 g ricotta, fresh semisoft farmer's cheese, or Mexican queso fresco
1 large egg
Heaped 1 Tbsp finely chopped fresh cilantro
4 sheets phyllo dough or *warqa* (see page 46), plus more in case of breakage
Olive oil for brushing
1 egg yolk, whisked
Honey
Light olive oil or vegetable oil for frying
1 Tbsp toasted sesame seeds

In a medium mixing bowl, blend the cheese, egg, and cilantro with a fork.

On a clean, flat work surface, unroll the phyllo sheets. Cut into strips about 3 in/7.5 cm wide and at least 9 in/23 cm long. Arrange a couple of the strips facing away from you; cover the remaining strips with plastic wrap to keep them from drying out. Lightly brush the strips with olive oil.

Place 1 Tbsp of the cheese mixture on the end of each strip closest to you. Fold over to form a triangle, then fold again to form another triangle, and so on to the end. Brush the end of the triangle with egg yolk and fold the loose end over the brushed yolk. Place the triangles on a plate without letting them touch. Repeat with the remaining phyllo strips and cheese filling.

Have ready six dessert plates. Place a generous dollop of honey in the middle of each.

In a large skillet or sauté pan over high heat, heat at least ½ in/12 mm of oil until the surface shimmers. Reduce the heat to medium. Working in small batches, gently place the phyllo triangles in the oil and fry, turning once, until firm and golden brown, 30 seconds to 1 minute. Transfer with a slotted spoon to paper towels to drain.

Place two or three rolls on each plate, drizzle with honey, and sprinkle with the sesame seeds. Serve hot.

The classic stuffed Moroccan pastry called *pastilla* (also spelled *b'stilla* and variations in between) is filled with a rich mixture of pigeon or chicken, almonds, eggs, and cinnamon. A seafood version, with fish, shrimp, and calamari, as well as, perhaps surprisingly, thin Asian rice noodles, is modern, festive, and very popular. I have heard from a few people that it dates only from the 1990s, but by its integration into the Moroccan kitchen, that's hard to imagine.

Generally cooked in a skillet until golden and with slightly crispy edges, the *pastilla* can also be brushed with oil and baked in the oven; both methods are given below.

SEAFOOD PASTILLA

MAKES ONE 8-IN/20-CM PASTILLA; SERVES 6 TO 8

Salt

1 lb/455 g firm white-fleshed fish fillets such as cod, bream, or monkfish

3 oz/85 g thin Asian rice stick noodles

4 Tbsp/60 ml olive oil, plus more for brushing pastry sheets

1 lb/455 g cleaned calamari, chopped

1 lb/455 g peeled uncooked shrimp

2 garlic cloves, minced

½ red bell pepper, seeded, deribbed, and finely chopped

½ green bell pepper, seeded, deribbed, and finely chopped

1 tsp grated lemon zest, or ½ preserved lemon (see page 45), flesh scraped out and discarded, peel finely chopped

Heaped 1 Tbsp finely chopped fresh flat-leaf parsley

Heaped 1 Tbsp finely chopped fresh cilantro

½ tsp sweet paprika

½ tsp ground cumin

1 pinch saffron threads, dry-toasted and ground (see page 50)

Freshly ground black pepper

8 sheets phyllo dough or *warqa* (see page 46), plus more in case of breakage

1 egg yolk, whisked

2 lemons, cut into wedges

In a large saucepan, bring at least 8 cups/2 L water to a boil and add a generous 2 pinches of salt. Reduce the heat to low, gently set the fish in the water, and poach until opaque throughout, about 5 minutes, depending on the thickness of the fillet. Carefully transfer with a slotted spoon to a platter to drain and cool.

In the same water, add the noodles and boil until tender but not mushy, about 3 minutes. Drain in a colander and rinse with hot water. Transfer to a large mixing bowl. Cut with scissors into shorter lengths.

Flake the fish, discarding the skin and any bones. Transfer to the bowl with the noodles.

In a large skillet or sauté pan, heat 2 Tbsp of the olive oil over high heat. Add the calamari and cook until it has released its moisture and is golden and tender, 5 to 10 minutes. Add the shrimp and cook until it has released its moisture, 5 to 10 minutes. Transfer to the mixing bowl.

Add the remaining 2 Tbsp oil to the skillet and reduce the heat to medium. Add the garlic and cook until fragrant and golden, about 1 minute. Add the red and green bell peppers, and cook until soft, about 5 minutes. Add the lemon zest, parsley, cilantro, paprika, cumin, and saffron and season with salt and pepper. Return the seafood mixture to the pan and turn to blend. Return to the mixing bowl. Taste for seasoning and adjust as needed.

Lay a sheet of the phyllo over a standard 9-in/23-cm pie or cake pan or round baking dish. Lightly brush with olive oil and lay another phyllo sheet on top of the first, somewhat overlapping. Lightly brush with oil and repeat with two more sheets so that there are four total, with each one somewhat overlapping the other. Spoon the seafood mixture evenly over the center.

Fold the corners of the phyllo over the top. Top with one phyllo sheet, brush with oil, and lay another sheet on top, somewhat overlapping. Brush with oil and repeat with the remaining two sheets. Invert the *pastilla* onto a plate. Brush the edges of the phyllo with the egg yolk and fold over, working in a clockwise manner to bring up the bottom sheets and enclose the *pastilla*.

To cook the *pastilla* in a skillet, lightly brush the *pastilla* with olive oil, place in an 8- or 9-in/ 20- or 23-cm skillet over medium-low heat and gently cook until the edges are golden and slightly crispy, about 10 minutes. Turn halfway through cooking by pressing an upturned plate over the skillet, carefully turning both the plate and skillet, and then sliding the *pastilla* back into the pan.

To bake the *pastilla* in the oven, preheat the oven to 300°F/150°C/gas mark 2. Line a baking sheet with parchment paper. Lightly brush the *pastilla* with oil, lay on the sheet, and bake until golden and the edges are slightly crispy, about 40 minutes. Turn about halfway through cooking.

Transfer to a serving plate, cut into wedges and serve hot with the lemons on the side.

This layered, square Berber flatbread is cooked in a skillet or on a griddle until the edges are golden brown. Drizzled with honey, a warm *rghayif* is a favorite for breakfast or a snack. Some in Morocco also turn the flatbread into a savory treat and eat it with preserved meat called *khlea* (see page 44).

LAYERED
BERBER FLATBREAD

rghayif

MAKES 8 TO 10 FLATBREADS

3¾ cups/500 g all-purpose flour
1 Tbsp salt
1¼ cups/300 ml warm water
Vegetable oil for moistening hands and
    work surface
20 or so coin-size pieces of butter
Coarse semolina for sprinkling
Honey for drizzling

In a wide mixing bowl or *gsâa*, sift in the flour. Mix in the salt and begin working in the water to form a compact ball.

Transfer to a clean, lightly floured surface and knead for 10 minutes until supple and elastic.

Moisten your hands with oil. Take some dough and squeeze it in the palm of a hand, forcing out a piece the size of a large plum through the thumb and forefinger. Pinch off and place on a plate. Repeat with the remaining dough to make 8 to 10 balls total. Cover with plastic wrap and let rest for 5 to 10 minutes.

On a flat, lightly oiled work surface, press each ball flat and begin working the dough outward with your hands to form an even round sheet about 15 in/38 cm in diameter. Place two pieces of butter in the middle and lightly sprinkle with semolina. Fold in two sides so that they overlap in the center and then fold in the other two sides, making a 4½- to 5-in/11.5- to 12.5-cm square. Lay on a baking sheet.

Heat a skillet or griddle over medium heat.

Lay each piece of folded dough on the oiled surface and press out to about 6 to 7 in/15 to 17 cm square. Sprinkle with a pinch of semolina and lay the dough, semolina-side down, in the skillet. Sprinkle with another pinch of semolina. Reduce the heat medium-low and cook until patchy golden, turning from time to time, about 5 minutes. Transfer to a platter lined with paper towels to absorb any excess oil.

Serve warm with honey for drizzling.

Bread is something so simple, so quotidian in Morocco. But at times, it's elevated to more than that. This bread, with pieces of black olives (ideally bold, salt-cured ones), coarsely ground walnuts, and sautéed onions, is adapted from one that a Marrakech *dada* (traditional family cook), Khadija Dilali, prepares for the year's main celebrations. It has a lovely burnished golden top from a brushing of egg yolk, is spongy on the inside, and exudes delectable savory aromas and flavors.

Khadija cooks in AnaYela, a small, sumptuous *riad* sunk deep in the residential northeast corner of Marrakech's medina. The owners strongly believe that preserving the medina involves more than conserving buildings. The medina is a living organism, with its people and their way of life, and they take an active part in its daily rhythms. That begins with baking bread—including this one—in a communal oven down the lane.

The bread is divine with an herbed butter. Slightly soften the butter and mix with chopped oregano, thyme, or rosemary, or a blend of all three.

BLACK OLIVE, WALNUT, AND ONION BREAD

MAKES FOUR 5- TO 6-IN/12- TO 15-CM LOAVES

3½ Tbsp olive oil
2 medium red onions, grated
1½ Tbsp/20 g firmly packed fresh baker's yeast
1 tsp sea salt
¾ cup/180 ml warm water
3¾ cups/500 g all-purpose flour
1 cup/100 g walnut pieces, roughly ground
¾ cup/100 g black olives, pitted and quartered
1 egg yolk, whisked

In a medium skillet or sauté pan, heat the olive oil over medium heat. Add the onions and cook until soft and translucent, about 12 minutes. Transfer to a bowl to cool.

In a small bowl, dissolve the yeast and salt in the water.

In a large mixing bowl or *gsâa*, sift in the flour and then blend in the walnuts, olives, and reserved onions. Form a dome with a well in the top and begin working in the yeast mixture, kneading until a compact ball forms. Add a touch more water if needed.

Transfer the dough to a clean, lightly floured surface and knead for 10 to 15 minutes until supple, elastic, and tacky to the touch.

Divide the dough into four even pieces and roll into slightly flattened balls. Lightly dust the tops with flour. Cover with a clean kitchen cloth and let rest for 10 minutes.

Line a baking sheet with parchment paper or lightly flour the sheet. Transfer the loaves to the prepared sheet, spacing them at least 2 in/5 cm apart. With the palm of a hand, flatten to about 1 in/2.5 cm thick. Lightly dust the tops with flour, if needed. Cover the loaves with a clean kitchen cloth and then with plastic wrap, and leave in a warm place to rise for 1 hour. The loaves are ready when the dough springs back after it is very lightly poked with finger.

Preheat the oven to 350°F/180°C/ gas mark 4.

Using a pastry brush, paint the top of the loaves with the egg yolk. Bake until golden and spongy, about 25 minutes. Rotate the pan halfway through baking. Cool the loaves on wire racks. Once completely cooled, store in a cloth bag until ready to serve. To keep longer than a day, wrap in plastic wrap or aluminum foil and freeze.

This is a smaller version of the straightforward and fairly standard, slightly domed loaves found throughout the country. Serve the bread, or another bread, with every savory recipe in the book. For a celebratory variation that is especially popular during Eid al-Adha festivities to accompany lamb dishes, blend 1 teaspoon orange flower water and 1 teaspoon toasted sesame seeds into the dough.

CLASSIC
ROUND BREAD

khobz

MAKES TWO 6-IN/15-CM LOAVES

3¾ cups/500 g all-purpose flour
1½ Tbsp/20 g firmly packed fresh baker's yeast
1 tsp sea salt
1 cup/240 ml plus 1 Tbsp warm water
Cornmeal or coarse semolina for sprinkling
    (optional)

In a large mixing bowl or *gsâa*, sift in the flour and form a dome with a well in the top. In a small bowl, dissolve the yeast and salt in the water. Gradually add to the flour, working the dough into a compact ball.

Transfer the dough to a clean, lightly floured surface and knead for 10 to 15 minutes until supple, elastic, and slightly tacky to the touch.

Divide the dough into two even pieces and roll into slightly flattened balls. Lightly dust the tops with flour. Cover with a clean kitchen cloth and let rest for 10 minutes.

Line a baking sheet with parchment paper or lightly flour the sheet. Transfer the loaves to the prepared sheet, spacing them at least 2 in/5 cm apart. With the palm of a hand, flatten to about 1 in/2.5 cm thick. Lightly dust the tops with flour, if needed. Cover the loaves with a clean kitchen cloth and then with plastic wrap, and leave in a warm place to rise for 1 hour. The loaves are ready when the dough springs back after it is very lightly poked with a finger.

Preheat the oven to 350°F/180°C/gas mark 4.

Firmly prick the loaves five or six times with the tines of a fork, and sprinkle with cornmeal, if desired. Bake until golden and hollow sounding when tapped, about 25 minutes. Rotate the pan halfway through baking. Cool the loaves on wire racks. Once completely cooled, store in a cloth bag until ready to serve. To keep longer than a day, wrap in plastic wrap or aluminum foil and freeze.

SOUPS
AND
LEGUMES

Soups are widely enjoyed in the cold, damp north, along the coast, across the central plains, in the mountains, and in the desert. One can talk about Moroccans' love for soups and about the amounts they prepare and devour, but not necessarily about variety. Two soups dominate the Moroccan table, and they are both legendary.

The first is *harira* (facing page), a smooth, tomato-based soup full of fresh herbs. While eaten year-round, it's the traditional dish to break the daily fast during the month of Ramadan. The second is *bessara* (page 77), a thick purée of dried fava beans or green split peas that is drizzled with olive oil and dusted with a sprinkle of cumin or paprika before serving.

Other cooked legumes—lentils (see page 78) and white beans (see page 79)—make excellent soups. Or, with less liquid, they can also be served as salads.

There are a number semolina-based Berber soups or, more accurately, porridges. One is the humble *lassida* (*tarwait* in Berber), served with a dollop of butter on top; when that disappears, *lben* (buttermilk) is poured into the bowl. Many variations can be found in the Anti-Atlas, with some including honey, in areas where beehives are kept, or saffron threads or aniseed. In the past, similar soups were frequently made from millet, but these days small-scale farmers plant less of the cereal. Millet—*anili* in Moroccan Arabic, *illane* in Berber—requires abundant water to grow and also takes longer to cook.

Harira is Morocco's best-known, and best-loved, soup. Families eat this herb-rich, tomato-based soup year-round. During Ramadan, however, it's obligatory, and pots of the soup simmer away in kitchens across the country. Accompanied by dates and honeyed, flower-shaped cookies sprinkled with sesame seeds called *chebakia*, a bowl of *harira* is the traditional way to break the fast. The velvety-smooth soup—whisking in flour, or sometimes egg, at the end gives that distinct texture—is nourishing and easy on an empty stomach.

I have enjoyed *harira* around numerous family tables and at street stalls—each version has been different. As a woman in Fès once said to me, "There are as many recipes for *harira* in Morocco as there are cooks."

HARIRA

SERVES 8

1 lb/455 g stewing beef, cut into ½-in/
    12-mm cubes

1 cup/170 g finely chopped celery stalks,
    tender green parts and leaves only

1 medium onion, finely chopped

⅓ cup/15 g loosely packed, finely chopped
    fresh flat-leaf parsley

⅓ cup/15 g loosely packed, finely chopped
    fresh cilantro

1 Tbsp butter, *smen* (see page 45), or olive oil

1 tsp ground ginger

½ tsp ground cinnamon

Salt and freshly ground black pepper

Two 14-oz/410-g cans peeled whole tomatoes,
    seeded and puréed with all the juices

3 Tbsp tomato paste

1 cup/170 g canned chickpeas, rinsed

¼ cup/30 g all-purpose flour

Juice of 1 lemon

1 oz/30 g vermicelli or angel hair pasta,
    broken into ¾-in/2-cm lengths

1 lemon, cut into wedges

12 dates, preferably *mejhoul*

12 dried figs

In a large soup pot, put the meat, celery, onion, parsley, cilantro, butter, ginger, and cinnamon. Season with salt and plenty of pepper. Cover with 6 cups/1.5 L water, stir well, and bring to a boil over high heat. Reduce the heat to low, cover, and simmer for 1 hour.

Add the tomatoes, tomato paste, and chickpeas, and stir in 1½ cups/360 ml water. Cover and simmer for 30 minutes.

Meanwhile, in a small saucepan over low heat, warm 1 cup/240 ml water and whisk in the flour and lemon juice. Remove from the heat, let sit for 10 minutes, and then whisk again.

Add the flour mixture to the soup in a slow but steady stream while continually stirring. Cook, stirring frequently to avoid any sticking, for 10 minutes. Sprinkle in the vermicelli and cook until the pasta is tender, about 5 minutes. The texture of the soup should be velvety.

Serve in bowls with lemon wedges on the side and with the dates and figs on a small platter.

This recipe comes from a damp, cold winter's dinner at Dar Nour—"House of Light"—inside Tanger's dense, whitewashed Kasbah. Into a dining room full of books, intimate photos of the city's rich literary history, patterned Berber textiles, European antiques, and flickering candles, the silky, scarlet soup was presented in a heavy white tureen. It was smooth and warmingly piquant with ginger and a generous grating of black pepper. Perfect!

Away from Tanger and its Mediterranean blues, I have been served very different versions of this soup. On a hot spring night at the edge of the vast palm groves in the southern oasis of Zagora, among dusty, pounded mud-and-straw *pisé* walls of an ancient house in the medina, the soup came slightly chilled and without the ginger, which allowed the earthy sweetness of the beets to come through stronger. That version tasted as perfect in Zagora as this warm, spicy version did in Tanger.

BEET SOUP
WITH
GINGER

SERVES 6 TO 8

1½ lb/680 g medium beets, peeled and
    quartered
1½ lb/680 g medium white potatoes,
    peeled and quartered
Salt and freshly ground black pepper
Scant ½ tsp ground ginger

In a medium pot over high heat, put the beets and potatoes, add 5½ cups/1.3 L water, and bring to a boil. Season with salt and pepper, cover, and cook at a low boil until the beets and potatoes are soft but not crumbling, 40 to 45 minutes.

Remove from the heat, remove the lid, and let cool, stirring occasionally, for about 10 minutes.

Using a food processor, and working in batches as needed, purée the soup for at least 1 minute until satiny smooth.

Return the soup to the pot and stir in the ginger. Bring almost to a boil over medium heat. Taste for seasoning and adjust as needed. Serve in white bowls to show off the vibrant color.

Bessara is a rustic, hearty soup much beloved in Morocco. The purée of cooked small dried split fava beans is a specialty of the Rif Mountains, where it's ladled into bowls and served with a drizzle of extra-virgin olive oil and a pinch of sweet paprika. In the northern part of the country, *bessara* is also made using dried green split peas.

The final consistency shouldn't be silky, but have a bit of texture. The soup is excellent with Classic Round Bread (page 68) or Black Olive, Walnut, and Onion Bread (page 66), and some sharp, salt-cured black olives. The mother of a friend in Rabat always serves her split pea *bessara* with panfried fresh sardines—another perfect combination.

SPLIT PEA SOUP WITH CUMIN AND PAPRIKA

bessara

SERVES 4

About 2 cups/450 g dried green split peas
6 garlic cloves
1 tsp ground cumin
½ tsp sweet paprika, plus more for garnishing
1 pinch cayenne pepper
Salt
Extra-virgin olive oil for drizzling

Pour the split peas into a large bowl. Pick over and remove any stones or debris. Rinse and drain.

In a medium pot over high heat, put the split peas and garlic. Add 7 cups/1.7 L water, stir, and bring to a boil. Skim off any foam. Reduce the heat to low, cover, and cook at a gentle boil until the split peas are tender, 45 minutes to 1 hour.

Remove from the heat, remove the lid, and let cool slightly, stirring occasionally. Pass the soup through a food mill. Or purée the soup in a food processor using quick pulses until it has a creamy but textured consistency. For soup with a coarser texture, mash by hand.

Return the soup to the pot and reheat over medium heat while stirring in the cumin, the ½ tsp paprika, and cayenne pepper. Season with salt. If the soup is too thin, reduce over medium heat to the desired consistency.

Ladle into bowls, garnish each with a drizzled circle of olive oil and a generous pinch of paprika, and serve.

Cooked lentils make a simple, hearty, and inexpensive meal eaten at home or from street-stall vendors. The fresh herbs, stirred in at the end, give the lentils an appealing earthiness as well as a vivid touch of color.

Lentils are often prepared as a cooked salad. To make this recipe as a salad, boil the lentils in the water with the onion until done but still firm, 25 to 35 minutes, then drain off any remaining liquid. Stir in the spices and olive oil, and top with the fresh herbs. Serve warm or at room temperature.

Moroccan markets sell two sizes of lentils: tiny brown ones and larger khaki green ones. The small ones are preferable here. Lentils do not need to be soaked before cooking.

SOUPY LENTILS

âades

SERVES 6

About 2 cups/400 g small brown lentils

1 medium onion, thinly sliced

2 ripe, medium tomatoes, halved, seeded, and grated (see Note)

2 garlic cloves, minced

1 Tbsp extra-virgin olive oil, plus more for drizzling

½ tsp ground cumin

¼ tsp sweet paprika

¼ tsp freshly ground black pepper

1 pinch saffron threads, dry-toasted (see page 50) and ground

Salt

Finely chopped fresh flat-leaf parsley for garnishing

Finely chopped fresh cilantro for garnishing

Pour the lentils into a large bowl. Pick over and remove any stones or debris. Rinse and drain.

In a medium pot, put the lentils, onion, tomatoes, garlic, olive oil, cumin, paprika, pepper, and saffron. Season with salt. Cover with 6 cups/1.5 L water, stir, and bring to a boil over high heat. Reduce the heat to low, cover, and cook at a low boil until the lentils are very tender but not mushy, 35 to 45 minutes. Add more water if necessary to keep the lentils loose and soupy or, alternatively, remove the lid to reduce some liquid. Taste for seasoning and adjust as needed.

Ladle into bowls, top each with a drizzle of olive oil and some parsley and cilantro, and serve.

NOTE: *To grate tomatoes, halve the tomatoes crosswise. Place a small strainer over a bowl. Seed the tomatoes by running a finger through the cavity and into the strainer in order to catch all of the juices. Cup a tomato half in the palm of your hand and grate on a box grater, working so that the skin gradually flattens back as the soft flesh of the tomato comes away. All that should be left is the skin.*

Stewed white beans in tomato sauce are especially popular in the north of the country, where they are eaten for lunch or dinner, as a salad or side dish, and by laborers as a substantial and economical breakfast. Directions for preparing with dried beans or with canned beans follow. Using canned ones makes this a quick dish to prepare. Serve with plenty of bread.

WHITE BEANS
IN
TOMATO SAUCE

loubia

SERVES 4 TO 6

About ¾ cup/140 g dried cannellini, borlotti, or other white beans, or a generous 2 cups/400 g canned white beans
3 Tbsp butter, *smen* (see page 45), or olive oil
1 medium red onion, finely chopped
3 garlic cloves, minced
2 ripe medium tomatoes, halved, seeded, and grated (see Note, facing page)
1 Tbsp finely chopped fresh flat-leaf parsley
1 Tbsp finely chopped fresh cilantro
½ tsp ground cumin
½ tsp sweet paprika
Salt and freshly ground black pepper

If using dried beans, soak them in water to cover overnight. Drain, rinse, and drain again. Put in a large pot, cover with plenty of cool water, and bring to a boil over high heat. Partly cover the pot and cook at a very gentle boil, shaking the pot from time to time, until the beans are tender but not mushy, 1½ to 2 hours. Remove from the heat. Drain only when ready to add to the tomato sauce.

If using canned beans, drain, rinse, and drain again. Put in a saucepan, cover with cool water, and bring to a boil over high heat. Remove from the heat. Drain only when ready to add to the tomato sauce.

In a medium skillet or sauté pan, melt the butter over medium-low heat. Add the onion and garlic and cook, stirring from time to time, until the onion is translucent and the garlic is colored, about 8 minutes. Add the tomatoes and cook, stirring from time to time, until they are a deeper red and pulpy, about 10 minutes. Add 1½ cups/360 ml water and bring to a boil. Cover and simmer for 10 minutes.

Drain the beans, discarding the liquid. Add the beans to the tomato sauce, sprinkle in the parsley, cilantro, cumin, and paprika and season with salt and pepper. Partially cover and cook for 10 to 15 minutes. The tomato sauce should be a bit runny. Splash in some water to keep it loose if necessary. Taste for seasoning and adjust as needed.

Ladle into bowls and serve.

STREET FOOD

Potato Fritters
maakouda
• 83 •

Chickpeas in Broth
• 84 •

Djemaa El Fna Snails in Broth
babbouche
• 85 •

Fried Marinated Sardine Pairs
serdine chrak
• 88 •

Grilled Sardines
• 91 •

Grilled Marinated Chicken Brochettes
• 92 •

Grilled Spicy Kefta Brochettes
• 94 •

Street food is one of the great culinary pleasures of Moroccan cities. Stalls sell plenty of dates, dried fruits, and nuts to munch on—almonds, walnuts, freshly roasted peanuts, dried figs, shiny black prunes, golden orange apricots, various sizes and colors of raisins. Freshly squeezed juices are abundant, and tea is always easy to find. The smell of grilling meats—skewers of marinated lamb or spiced, ground meat known as *kefta* (see page 94), marinated chicken (see page 92)—fills the small streets of medinas. Along the coast, the aroma comes from grilling sardines (see page 91), and in El Jadida from ears of corn as well. There are deep-fried potato fritters (see facing page), thick just-fried doughnuts called *sfenj*, bowls of chickpeas in broth (see page 84), and, most famously in Fès, stuffed spleen known as *tihane*. Something for all tastes.

On Marrakech's iconic square, Djemaa el Fna, as dusk falls, Moroccan street food rises to an art—or at least the ultimate experience. Among the jugglers, musicians, storytellers, snake charmers, and men from the deep south peddling ancient medicinal remedies, hundreds of food stalls sell everything from sandwiches with hard-boiled eggs to small grilled *merguez* sausages to a potent (and some think aphrodisiac) tea called *atay melouki* (King Tea) made with galanga root, cardamom, aniseed, licorice root, cinnamon, and pepper. There are steamed sheep heads paired with bowls of semolina soup dusted in cumin or caraway, pieces of deep-fried conger eel, and the famous bowls of snails in a rich, spice- and tea-laden broth (see page 85).

I imagine that this nightly scene, with its carnival atmosphere, is something like it once was in medieval times in front of Europe's great cathedrals during festivals. But in Marrakech, it happens every day.

Hot deep-fried fritters, boldly spiced with cumin, turmeric, garlic, fresh herbs, and perhaps some red pepper flakes, are a specialty of Fès's ancient medina. They are eaten alone or tucked into a pocket of bread.

The trick to making them is to get the fritters to hold their shape. Work a small amount of flour into the mix—the minimum, just enough so that the fritters will hold together—and use well-floured hands when forming patties. Prepare and fry the fritters in small batches, or have two pairs of hands—one pair making patties, the other frying them—in order to serve them hot.

POTATO FRITTERS

maakouda

MAKES 16 TO 20 FRITTERS

2 lb/910 g medium white rose potatoes, peeled and quartered

Salt

1 medium red onion

2 large eggs

1 Tbsp finely chopped fresh flat-leaf parsley

1 Tbsp finely chopped fresh cilantro

1 tsp ground cumin

½ tsp turmeric

Freshly ground black pepper

Red pepper flakes

All-purpose flour as needed

Light olive oil or vegetable oil for frying

In a large saucepan over medium-high heat, boil the potatoes in lightly salted water until done but still firm, about 20 minutes. Transfer to a colander to drain and cool.

Meanwhile, grate the onion and place in a strainer to drain off any excess moisture. Push down on the onion to squeeze out any liquid.

In a small bowl, whisk the eggs with the parsley, cilantro, cumin, and turmeric. Season with salt, pepper, and red pepper flakes. Add the onion and potatoes and gently blend.

Put flour in a small mixing bowl.

Take a small handful of the potato mixture and work in just enough flour so that the mixture will hold its shape. With floured hands, form into a patty about 3 in/7.5 cm in diameter. Place on a platter and form patties with the remaining mixture.

In a large skillet, heat at least ½ in/12 mm of oil over high heat until the surface shimmers. Reduce the heat to medium. Working in small batches, slide the patties into the oil and fry until golden brown, turning once, about 1 minute or less on each side. Transfer with a slotted spoon to paper towels to drain. Serve hot.

Like many of the hot dishes found in street stalls, small bowls of chickpeas in broth are inexpensive and filling, and usually eaten standing up. The raisins here give a nice sweet touch. For a spicy version, replace the raisins with a pinch of cayenne pepper or red pepper flakes. Prepared with canned chickpeas, this is a quick and easy dish to make at home.

Another favorite way to prepare chickpeas on the street is steaming them until warm and tender and dusting them with paprika, cumin, and salt. This makes an even quicker snack.

CHICKPEAS IN BROTH

SERVES 4

2 Tbsp olive oil
1 medium red onion, grated
About 2½ cups/400 g canned chickpeas
Scant ¼ cup/30 g raisins
½ tsp sweet paprika
½ tsp ground cumin
Salt and freshly ground black pepper
Finely chopped fresh cilantro for garnishing

In a large saucepan, heat the olive oil over medium heat. Add the onion and cook until translucent, 5 to 8 minutes.

Rinse the chickpeas well, drain, and add to the pan. Add the raisins, paprika, and cumin and season with salt and pepper. Stir well, cover with 2 cups/480 ml water, and bring to a boil. Reduce the heat to low, cover, and simmer until the chickpeas are tender.

Ladle into bowls with some of the broth, sprinkle each bowl with a pinch of cilantro, and serve.

Snails are a street-stall staple, especially in Marrakech on Djemaa el Fna square, where a line of sturdy carts sells them by the broth-filled bowl. The flavorful broth sipped at the end is said to be a restorative and digestive. But what's in it? One respected *attar* (spice seller) in Marrakech gave me a list of more than fifteen spices from thyme and licorice to lavender and tea leaves. "Which are the most important?" I asked. "They all are," he said. "The balance has to be right."

Here I have adapted the spice blend of Choumicha, the queen of contemporary Moroccan cooking. It's a relatively simple one, but flavorful and balanced.

Moroccan snails are white with distinctive chocolate brown whirls, smaller than the classic French *escargot*. Live snails added to boiling water will retract inside the shell and be hard to remove later to eat. When the snails are first cooked, it's important to bring the water to a very slow boil. While live snails can be hard to find, many gourmet shops carry preserved ones in cans.

DJEMAA EL FNA

SNAILS IN BROTH

babbouche

SERVES 4 TO 6

2 lb/910 g fresh snails or snails in brine
Salt
Wine vinegar or other vinegar for
   cleaning snails
2 sprigs dried thyme
½ Tbsp aniseed
½ Tbsp caraway seeds
½ tsp gunpowder green tea leaves
Peel from ½ orange, white pith scraped away
Two 3-in/7.5-cm pieces licorice root
   (see page 50) or 1 tsp ground aniseed
2 bay leaves
½ tsp dried mint
10 sprigs fresh mint
2 small dried hot red chiles

If using live snails, wash with plenty of water. Use salt and vinegar to scrub clean if the shells are dirty. Repeat as needed. Rinse well. Put the snails in a large pot with about 3 qt/2.8 L water. Bring to a slow boil over low heat—figure about 45 minutes for this—watching to keep the snails inside the pot. When the water reaches a boil and foam comes to the surface, drain the snails in a colander. Rinse the snails well with running water and rinse out the pot.

=== CONTINUED ===

If using snails preserved in brine, drain the brine and rinse the snails well. In a large pot, add the snails and cover with water. Bring to a boil over high heat and boil for 5 minutes. Drain the snails in a colander. Rinse the snails well with running water and rinse out the pot.

Return the snails to the pot. Cover with 8 cups/2 L water, and add the thyme, aniseed, caraway seeds, tea leaves, orange peel, licorice root, bay leaves, dried mint, and fresh mint.

Season with a pinch of salt. Bring to a boil over high heat, reduce the heat to medium-low, loosely cover, and simmer for 1½ hours. The snails should be tender and the broth rich and flavorful. Add the chiles and cook for 10 minutes. Taste the broth and adjust the seasoning as needed.

Serve the snails hot in bowls with some broth. Use a toothpick to extract the snails from their shells.

As Morocco is the world's sardine capital, it comes as no surprise that this small, healthful fish is eaten frequently and in many different dishes. One popular way to prepare sardines on the street is with a garlic-and-herb-laden *charmoula* marinade smeared between two facing butterflied sardines, which are then lightly floured and deep-fried as a pair. They are called *serdine chrak*. *Chrak* means "coupled" or "partnered." They are also sometimes known by the amorous French term, *sardines amoureuses*.

Marinated pairs can also be panfried, grilled, covered with tomato sauce and baked, or prepared in a tagine. But deep-frying the fish in a big, blackened kettle of bubbling oil is the classic street style. Shake off as much flour as possible before slipping the pairs into the hot oil.

Note that Atlantic sardines tend to be larger than their Mediterranean counterparts and may require more marinade.

FRIED MARINATED
SARDINE PAIRS

serdine chrak

MAKES 12 PAIRS; SERVES 4 TO 6

24 medium sardines

4 garlic cloves, minced

Heaped 2 Tbsp finely chopped fresh flat-leaf parsley

Heaped 2 Tbsp finely chopped fresh cilantro

1 tsp ground cumin

1 tsp sweet paprika

¼ tsp cayenne pepper or red pepper flakes

Salt and freshly ground black pepper

¼ cup/60 ml fresh lemon juice

1 Tbsp olive oil

Light olive oil or vegetable oil for deep-frying

All-purpose flour for dredging

2 lemons, cut into wedges

Rinse the sardines and clean each. Remove the head, trim the tail, and gently open outward, sliding a thumbnail along the central spine to remove it, as well as any bones. Spread open into a single, butterflied fillet.

In a small mixing bowl, add the garlic, parsley, cilantro, cumin, paprika, and cayenne. Season with salt and pepper. Moisten with the lemon juice and 1 Tbsp olive oil. Blend well.

Coat the sardines with the marinade and lay in a shallow bowl. Spoon the remaining marinade over the fish. Cover and marinate for at least 15 minutes.

Lay a sardine skin-side down. Spread with 1½ tsp of the marinade and then place a second sardine on top skin-side up. Repeat with the remaining sardines and marinade.

In a large skillet or sauté pan, heat at least ½ in/12 mm of oil over high heat until the surface shimmers. Reduce the heat to medium-high.

Put flour in a wide bowl. Holding a sardine pair together, coat with flour and then dust off any excess. With a slotted spoon or spatula, gently slip the pair into the oil. Cook until golden, 30 seconds to 1 minute. Transfer to paper towels to drain. Working in small batches, dust the remaining sardine pairs with flour and cook in the same manner.

Serve hot with the lemon wedges.

Fresh sardines grilling over embers, with salty oils dripping on the coals and sending clouds of aromatic smoke billowing upward, create one of the most evocative smells along the Atlantic coast, especially in Safi and El Jadida. This is robustly flavored finger food at its best.

Do not wash, scale, or clean the sardines! Be careful when handling the fish so that the scales don't flake off. Not only is the skin loaded with oils and flavor, but it is an important protective layer when the fish are grilled. Because sardines are difficult to turn without the skin sticking to the grill, they are usually placed in a grill basket. Sardines can also be prepared under a broiler. Lining the baking sheet with parchment paper is the most effective way to keep the skin intact when the fish are turned.

Serve the grilled sardines with an array of salads, plenty of fresh bread, and, perhaps, small bowls of fresh tomato dipping sauce (see page 158). Calculate six to ten sardines per person. Note that Atlantic sardines tend to be slightly larger than their Mediterranean counterparts.

GRILLED SARDINES

SERVES 4

24 to 40 fresh sardines
Coarse sea salt

If using a barbecue, prepare a fire and heat until the coals are glowing. Place the sardines in a grill basket, alternating the direction of the heads and tails. Liberally sprinkle both sides with salt.

Place the rack just above the coals and set the grill basket on the rack. Grill the sardines, fanning the embers to keep them hot, until the skin is buckled and charred and the eyes have gone white, turning various times, about 6 minutes total, depending on the size of the sardines. Carefully remove the fish from the grill basket. Grill the remaining sardines in batches.

If using a broiler, preheat the broiler. Line a baking sheet with parchment paper. Place the sardines on the sheet, spacing them about 1 in/2.5 cm apart. Liberally sprinkle with salt. Place a rack as close as possible to the heat source. Slide the baking sheet under the broiler. Broil the fish, turning once by gently rolling them over with the help of a spatula, until the skin is buckled and charred and the eyes have gone white, about 6 minutes total, depending on the size of the sardines. Carefully transfer to a platter. Reline the sheet with new parchment paper and broil the remaining sardines in batches, changing the parchment paper each time.

Serve immediately.

Like Grilled Spicy Kefta Brochettes (page 94), these are a favorite throughout the country, referred to as *snacks* in street stalls and in simple cafés. They're inexpensive, flavorful, and quick to prepare. The chicken takes on a lovely golden hue from the cumin and sweet paprika. Calculate about four brochettes per person as part of a meal, accompanied by a few salads and plenty of bread.

GRILLED MARINATED
CHICKEN BROCHETTES

MAKES ABOUT 16 BROCHETTES; SERVES 4

Heaped 2 Tbsp finely chopped fresh cilantro
2 tsp ground cumin
1 tsp sweet paprika
½ tsp cayenne pepper (optional)
Salt and freshly ground black pepper
6 Tbsp/90 ml olive oil
4 boneless, skinless chicken breasts (about 2 lb/
910 g), cut into ¾- to 1-in/2- to 2.5-cm cubes

In a large mixing bowl, add the cilantro, cumin, paprika, and cayenne (if using). Generously season with salt and pepper. Moisten with the olive oil and blend well. Add the chicken and turn to coat. Cover, refrigerate, and marinate for 1 hour, turning occasionally.

Prepare skewers with six to eight cubes of chicken on each. The pieces should be just touching, but not squashed tightly together.

If using a grill pan, skillet, or griddle, lightly oil and heat over medium-high heat. If using a barbecue, prepare a fire and heat until the coals are glowing. If using a broiler, preheat the broiler.

Cook the brochettes, nudging them from time to time with the help of a spatula in order to cook evenly on all sides, until the meat is cooked through and firm to touch, 4 to 5 minutes. Serve hot.

This favorite of street stalls, simple cafés, and roadside stops is ideal for a casual meal for friends. Serve with a selection of fresh and cooked salads, such as Cucumbers in Sweet Marinade with Oregano (page 99) and Chilled Sweet Butternut Squash Salad with Cinnamon (page 108). Calculate three brochettes per person.

Many Moroccan butchers sell *kefta* already seasoned with their own special blend of herbs and spices. To the standards—paprika, cumin, cinnamon, parsley, and cilantro—some include coriander seeds or mace and, in places like Azrou in the Middle Atlas, fresh mint.

GRILLED SPICY
KEFTA BROCHETTES

MAKES ABOUT 18 BROCHETTES; SERVES 6

1½ lb/680 g ground beef or lamb or a mix of the two (see Note)

1 medium red onion, finely grated

¼ cup/10 g loosely packed finely chopped fresh flat-leaf parsley

¼ cup/10 g loosely packed finely chopped fresh cilantro

Heaped 1 Tbsp finely chopped fresh mint (optional)

Generous 1 Tbsp sweet paprika

1 tsp ground cumin

1 tsp ground cinnamon

½ tsp ground mace or ⅛ tsp ground nutmeg

Generous 1 pinch cayenne pepper or red pepper flakes

Salt

Olive oil

In a large mixing bowl, blend the meat, onion, parsley, cilantro, mint (if using), paprika, cumin, cinnamon, mace, and cayenne. Season with salt. Unless the meat is quite fatty, work in a few drops of olive oil.

Take an egg-size handful of the mixture and press it around the middle of a skewer. Place on a clean, flat work surface and roll it lightly with the palms of your hands to form an even "sausage" 6 to 8 in/15 to 20 cm long. Pinch down both ends around the skewer. Gently set on a platter, and repeat with the remaining mixture.

If using a grill pan or griddle, lightly oil and heat over high heat. If using a barbecue, prepare a fire and heat until the coals are glowing. If using a broiler, preheat the broiler.

Cook the brochettes, nudging them from time to time with the help of a spatula in order to cook evenly on all sides, until the meat is cooked through and firm to touch, about 10 minutes. Serve hot.

NOTE: *The meat should have a bit of fat. If, once ground, it feels a bit dry, a few drops of olive oil will help moisten it. Have the butcher grind the meat twice. Some Moroccans blend in fat from around the kidney of a lamb, or, for its rich flavor, the kidney itself.*

FRESH AND COOKED
SALADS

Cucumbers in Sweet Marinade
with Oregano
• 99 •

Marinated Olives
zeytun m'charmel
• 100 •

Grated Carrot and Orange Salad
• 102 •

Carrot and Cumin Salad
• 103 •

Spicy Eggplant, Tomato,
and Garlic Salad
zaâlouk
• 105 •

Cooked Zucchini
and Tomato Salad
• 106 •

Flame-Grilled Green Pepper
and Fresh Tomato Salad
tchektchouka
• 107 •

Chilled Sweet
Butternut Squash Salad
with Cinnamon
• 108 •

Beet Salad with Green Onions
and Fresh Herbs
• 110 •

Serving an ample selection of what can be loosely called *salads* is one of Morocco's most delectable culinary traits. They offer an ideal showcase for the variety of flavors and colors of Moroccan cuisine and its sophisticated vegetarian traditions.

Salads can be divided into "fresh"—that is, uncooked, such as Grated Carrot and Orange Salad (page 102) and Cucumbers in Sweet Marinade with Oregano (facing page)—and "cooked," such as Carrot and Cumin Salad (page 103) and Chilled Sweet Butternut Squash Salad with Cinnamon (page 108). In general, cooked salads can be served chilled during the warmer months and at room temperature or even warm during cooler ones.

A course of salads sometimes precedes the main course, but in many homes they are placed on the table at the same time as, say, a tagine or roasted chicken. As everyone eats the main dish, they take a bit from this bowl of Beet Salad with Green Onions and Fresh Herbs (page 110), some Spicy Eggplant, Tomato, and Garlic Salad (page 105) from that one, and a spoonful of Flame-Grilled Green Pepper and Fresh Tomato Salad (page 107) from that other one. Delightful!

Cucumber salads are frequently prepared by grating the cucumber, which yields an almost soupy consistency. I prefer the firmer texture of this version (pictured on the bottom-left of page 96) with crunchy slices. A dusting of dried Moroccan wild oregano called *zaâtar* gives a savory edge to the sweet acidity of the sugar and lemon juice. Standard oregano makes a fine substitution. Add a pinch of thyme, if desired.

CUCUMBERS IN SWEET MARINADE WITH OREGANO

SERVES 4

1 Tbsp extra-virgin olive oil

2 tsp fresh lemon juice

1 Tbsp superfine sugar

Scant 1 tsp dried oregano or *zaâtar* (see page 48)

Salt

2 medium cucumbers, peeled and cut into thin rounds

24 black olives, preferably salt-cured with pits, rinsed

In a mixing bowl, whisk the olive oil, lemon juice, and sugar until the sugar dissolves. Add the oregano and season with salt. Add the cucumbers and turn gently to coat.

Cover with plastic wrap and chill for at least 1 hour until the flavors meld.

Transfer the cucumbers to a serving bowl. Spoon any remaining marinade on top. Garnish with the olives and serve.

Surely one of the most striking sights in a Moroccan *souq* is the precariously stacked displays of glistening olives, ranging in color from yellows and greens to violet purples and blacks. Stalls usually have their own herb- and spice-marinated versions, too, as do many restaurants, cafés, and even homes.

This recipe is adapted from the one that Rachid Edhidi, the talented barman at La Maison Arabe in Marrakech, mixes up in a silver Champagne bucket, chills, and then sets out with small, crunchy almonds (from the Atlas) on the dimpled zinc bar. The olives are delicious with a cold bottle of local Casablanca beer or, as Rachid prefers, for a midmorning or afternoon snack with just-baked bread and a glass of Mint Tea (page 210).

The first hot-water soak is important to remove some of the vinegary flavor so that the herby, spicy tones come through cleanly. Small pitted, unstuffed olives are preferable because the flavors can permeate deeper.

MARINATED OLIVES

zeytun m'charmel

MAKES ABOUT 2 CUPS/225 G OLIVES

2 cups/225 g pitted green olives or about 10 oz/280 g green olives with pits
1 small garlic clove, minced
Generous 2 pinches finely chopped fresh cilantro
Generous 2 pinches minced fresh rosemary
Generous 2 pinches dried oregano, *zaâtar* (see page 48), or dried thyme
Generous 2 pinches celery salt
Generous 2 pinches ground cumin
Generous 2 pinches freshly ground black pepper
Generous 2 pinches sea salt
Dash of Tabasco sauce
1½ Tbsp extra-virgin olive oil
1 tsp fresh lemon juice

Drain and rinse the olives. Transfer to a bowl, cover with hot water, and soak for 10 minutes. Rinse and let drain for 10 minutes. Spread out on paper towels to dry completely.

In a mixing bowl, blend the garlic, cilantro, rosemary, oregano, celery salt, cumin, pepper, salt, Tabasco, and olive oil.

Transfer the olives to a serving bowl. Add the herb mixture and stir evenly to coat. Cover with plastic wrap and refrigerate until chilled.

Add the lemon juice and toss. Serve chilled with toothpicks stuck into a handful of the olives.

Combining carrots and oranges, seasoned with orange flower water and cinnamon, is a frequently served favorite in Morocco. The salad should be just moist enough to need a spoon to eat it. The key to this dish (pictured at the top left of page 96) is grating the carrots very finely so that they can absorb the orange juice and soften slightly. For a version with more texture, add a few pieces of chopped orange segments, or grate the oranges instead of juicing them.

GRATED CARROT
AND
ORANGE SALAD

SERVES 6

½ lb/225 g medium carrots, scrubbed
2 medium oranges
1 Tbsp superfine sugar
1 dash orange flower water
Salt
Ground cinnamon for dusting

Cut each carrot lengthwise down the center and remove the core if it is tough. Grate the carrots as finely as possible. Transfer to a serving bowl. Juice the oranges and pour over the carrots.

Add the sugar, orange flower water, and a pinch of salt and mix well. Cover with plastic wrap and refrigerate for at least 2 hours.

Serve chilled in small bowls with spoons, dusted liberally with cinnamon.

A particular favorite around Marrakech and in the south, this cooked salad offers a delightful contrast of cold sweet carrots, earthy cumin, and fresh parsley. It's even better when prepared a day ahead and left overnight to chill and the flavors to fully meld. Set out alongside a bowl of Marinated Olives (page 100) to nibble on as an appetizer, or serve as part of a spread of salads.

CARROT
AND
CUMIN SALAD

SERVES 4 TO 6

1 lb/455 g medium carrots, scrubbed and
    cut into ¼-in-/6-mm-thick rounds
Salt
¼ cup/60 ml olive oil
1 tsp ground cumin
½ tsp sweet paprika
Freshly ground black pepper
½ tsp sugar
1 small lemon, halved
Heaped 2 Tbsp finely chopped fresh
    flat-leaf parsley

In a medium saucepan, boil the carrots in lightly salted water until just tender, 8 to 10 minutes. Fill a large mixing bowl with cold water.

Transfer the carrots with a slotted spoon to the cold water to stop further cooking. Once the carrots are cooled, remove with the slotted spoon and drain for a few minutes. Spread out on paper towels to dry completely.

In a large skillet or sauté pan, heat the olive oil over medium heat. Add the carrots, cumin, and paprika; season with pepper; and sprinkle with the sugar. Cook, stirring gently, for 1 minute. Remove from the heat. Squeeze half of the lemon over the carrots and sprinkle with the parsley. Turn the carrots to coat evenly.

Transfer to a bowl and let cool. Cover with plastic wrap and refrigerate until chilled.

Just before serving, squeeze the remaining lemon half over the carrots and turn to coat.

Morocco's most classic cooked salad, *zaâlouk* is surely its most popular. This dish can be served cold, warm, or at room temperature. For a smoky flavor, stir in some chopped, flame-roasted sweet green Italian or bell peppers. (See Flame-Grilled Green Pepper and Fresh Tomato Salad, page 107, for directions on preparing the peppers.)

SPICY EGGPLANT, TOMATO, AND GARLIC SALAD

zaâlouk

SERVES 6

3 medium eggplants (about 2 lb/910 g)
6 unpeeled garlic cloves
½ cup/120 ml extra-virgin olive oil
3 ripe medium tomatoes, peeled, seeded, and chopped, juices reserved
¼ tsp sweet paprika
1 pinch cayenne pepper or red pepper flakes
Salt and freshly ground black pepper
Heaped 1 Tbsp finely chopped fresh flat-leaf parsley

Trim each eggplant. Using a vegetable peeler or knife, remove a strip of skin, then leave a band of skin in place, and then remove another strip of skin, and so on. Quarter the eggplant lengthwise and then cut into 1- to 1½-in/2.5- to 4-cm pieces.

Put the eggplant and garlic in a steamer basket over at least 2 in/5 cm of water in a saucepan. Cover the eggplant snugly with foil and bring the water to a boil over high heat. Steam the eggplant until soft, about 25 minutes. Remove the garlic and let cool. Squeeze the garlic from the peels; discard the peels.

In a large skillet or sauté pan, heat the olive oil over medium heat and add the tomatoes, garlic, paprika, and cayenne. Season with salt and pepper. Cook, stirring frequently, until the tomatoes are a deeper red and pulpy, about 10 minutes. Stir in the eggplant. Cover and cook over medium heat, stirring and mashing down the ingredients frequently, until pasty, about 20 minutes.

Taste for seasoning and adjust as needed. Transfer to a serving bowl. Scatter with the parsley and serve.

In this salad full of distinctive contrasts, the tomatoes cook down until pulpy and rich, while the zucchini is added at the end and cooks briefly so that it remains a bit crunchy. The cilantro and cumin contribute an earthiness, while the black olives offer a vibrancy.

COOKED
ZUCCHINI AND
TOMATO SALAD

SERVES 4

¼ cup/60 ml extra-virgin olive oil
6 garlic cloves, minced
4 ripe plum tomatoes, seeded and chopped
Salt
½ Tbsp finely chopped fresh flat-leaf parsley
½ Tbsp finely chopped fresh cilantro
¼ tsp ground cumin
¼ tsp sweet paprika
1 pinch cayenne pepper
1 pinch freshly ground black pepper
1 lb/455 g zucchini, peeled, quartered lengthwise, and cut into ½-in/12-mm cubes
12 black olives with pits, rinsed
¼ lemon

In a large skillet or sauté pan, heat the olive oil over medium heat. Add the garlic and tomatoes and season with salt. Cook, stirring frequently, until the tomatoes are a deeper red and pulpy, about 10 minutes.

Sprinkle in the parsley, cilantro, cumin, paprika, cayenne, and pepper and stir well. Add the zucchini and olives. Cook, stirring from time to time, until the zucchini is tender but not mushy and still has a bite, about 5 minutes. Transfer to a serving bowl.

Serve at room temperature. Before serving, squeeze the lemon over the top and toss.

This classic salad mixes the smokiness of grilled peppers with the ripe freshness of tomatoes. You can grill the peppers over the open flame on a gas stove, on a charcoal grill, or under a broiler. Serve the salad at room temperature or chilled. For a zesty touch, stir in a tablespoon of finely chopped preserved lemon (see page 45).

FLAME-GRILLED GREEN PEPPER AND FRESH TOMATO SALAD

tchektchouka

SERVES 4

2 medium green bell peppers or 4 sweet Italian green peppers

3 ripe medium tomatoes, seeded and cut into ½-in-/12-mm cubes

2 small garlic cloves, minced

2 Tbsp finely chopped fresh flat-leaf parsley

2 Tbsp finely chopped fresh cilantro

1 pinch ground cumin

1 pinch sweet paprika

Salt and freshly ground black pepper

2 Tbsp extra-virgin olive oil

1 Tbsp fresh lemon juice

Wash the bell peppers and wipe dry with a paper towel.

To roast the peppers over a flame, impale them with a long fork or carving fork in the stem end and hold over a high-heat flame, turning from time to time, until the skin bubbles and blackens, about 8 minutes.

To roast the peppers on a grill, prepare a charcoal fire. When the coals are red and hot, grill the peppers, turning from time to time, until the skin bubbles and blackens, about 10 minutes.

To broil the peppers, preheat the broiler. Place the peppers on the top rack and broil, turning from time to time, until the skin bubbles and blackens, about 15 minutes.

Place the blackened peppers in a plastic bag and close, or wrap snugly in plastic wrap. Let soften and cool for 10 minutes. Working under running water, rub off the blackened skin. Remove the stems and seeds, and cut the peppers into ½-in-/12-mm-square pieces.

In a bowl, add the roasted peppers, tomatoes, garlic, parsley, cilantro, cumin, and paprika. Season with salt and pepper. Add the olive oil and lemon juice and toss to blend well before serving.

This chilled, cooked salad goes particularly well with grilled meats, especially Grilled Spicy Kefta Brochettes (page 94) and Grilled Marinated Chicken Brochettes (page 92). When cleaning the squash, be sure to scrape away all the stringy fibers and, when cutting, try to keep the cubes about the same size to ensure even cooking.

CHILLED SWEET
BUTTERNUT SQUASH
SALAD WITH CINNAMON

SERVES 4

2 lb/910 g butternut squash, acorn squash, pumpkin, or another firm-fleshed, hard-skinned squash

3 Tbsp olive oil

¼ cup/60 g sugar

2 pinches salt

½ tsp orange flower water or rose water

Ground cinnamon for dusting

1 tsp toasted sesame seeds

4 thin orange slices, halved, for garnishing

Cut the rind from the squash with a heavy, sharp knife, and scoop out the seeds. Cut the flesh into ½- to ¾-in/12-mm to 2-cm cubes.

In a large skillet or sauté pan, heat the olive oil over medium-high heat. Add the squash, sugar, and salt and cook, stirring from time to time, for 10 minutes. Sprinkle with the orange flower water, reduce the heat to medium, and cook until the squash is tender but not mushy, about 10 minutes.

Transfer to a serving bowl and let cool. Cover with plastic wrap and refrigerate until chilled.

Just before serving, lightly dust with cinnamon, sprinkle with the sesame seeds, and garnish with the orange slices.

A favorite vegetable in Morocco, the deep ruby beet is the star ingredient in this salad (pictured on the bottom-right of page 96) as well as a delicious soup (see page 74). The earthy sweetness of the beets in this dish is heightened with lemon juice and given an herby freshness with parsley and cilantro. The salad will delight even those who rarely eat beets.

BEET SALAD
WITH GREEN ONIONS
AND FRESH HERBS

SERVES 4

3 medium beets (about 1¼ lb/570 g)

3 Tbsp fresh lemon juice

3 Tbsp extra-virgin olive oil

Salt and freshly ground black pepper

2 Tbsp finely chopped fresh flat-leaf parsley

2 Tbsp finely chopped fresh cilantro

4 green onions, trimmed and cut crosswise into thin slices

Gently wash the beets but do not peel. To prevent the beets from "bleeding" while cooking, leave at least 1 in/2.5 cm of stems and do not trim the root ends.

In a medium pot over high heat, add the beets, cover with at least 2 in/5 cm of water, and bring to a boil. Reduce the heat to low, cover, and gently boil until the beets are tender and a knife tip can easily penetrate them, about 45 minutes. Drain in a colander and let cool.

Peel or slip off the skins and discard. Cut the beets into ½- to ¾-in/12-mm to 2-cm cubes and transfer to a salad bowl.

In a small mixing bowl, whisk the lemon juice and olive oil and season with salt and pepper. Blend in the parsley, cilantro, and green onions. Pour over the beets and then turn with a spoon until coated. Cover and refrigerate for 1 hour before serving.

MEATS

Lamb Tagine with
Sweetened Onions
• 115 •

Lamb Tagine with Oranges,
Saffron, and Candied Orange Peel
• 116 •

Salty-Sweet Glazed Lamb
with Almonds and Raisins
m'rouzia
• 119 •

Lamb with Garlic, Cumin,
and Coriander
mkila
• 120 •

Roast Lamb with Cumin
mechoui
• 121 •

Kid Tagine with Dried Figs
and Thyme
• 122 •

Sweet Veal Shank Tagine
with Caramelized Prunes
and Apricots
• 124 •

Veal Shank Tagine with Pears
• 126 •

Veal Shank Tagine with Peas
• 127 •

Kefta Meatball Tagine
in Tomato Sauce with Eggs
• 128 •

Marrakech Tangia
tangia
• 129 •

From the familiar scene of sheep grazing in fields and on hillsides across the country, it is clear that lamb is Morocco's most prevalent meat. Beef and goat are also widely used in the kitchen, while in the deep south, camel is the most common meat available. The rich, fine-grained meat is smooth in flavor and quite similar to beef. Treated the same way as beef or lamb, it is prepared in tagines and couscous, grilled, and ground into *kefta*.

The most important method for preparing meat is slow cooking it in a tagine. In its place, you can use a shallow, heavy, flameproof casserole; a Dutch oven; a braiser pan; or a large, heavy skillet or sauté pan. The conical lid of a tagine is usually not fully closed, but is left slightly ajar or opened a crack by propping a wooden spoon between the lid and the base of the tagine. The lid is lifted as needed to allow liquid to evaporate and the sauce to thicken. For more information on cooking with tagines, see page 55.

Lamb, kid, and veal are generally interchangeable in these stews and tagines. In each dish, I call for what is the most common. For slow-cooked or braised dishes, it's important to chose the right cut of meat for flavor and also to avoid allowing it to become dry by the end of cooking. Use a cut on the bone, such as the leg or shoulder for lamb. For veal, look for center-cut shanks with the round bone, a cut sometimes called osso buco.

This straightforward but divine sweet-and-savory tagine comes from the western foothills of the High Atlas, where scattered villages sprout organically from rusty red hills. The solid clay color of the houses is broken only by the white paint around a window or the occasional electric blue carpet draped over a sill to dry in the sun. A young Berber chef, Habiba Irich, prepared this tagine for me one late spring day. She laid thick slices of onions on top of the lamb, sprinkled them with sugar and cinnamon, and left the tagine to cook slowly on a charcoal brazier. We sipped glasses of an aromatic infusion of wild herbs from the hills above us until the onions draped meltingly soft over the succulent lamb.

LAMB TAGINE
WITH
SWEETENED ONIONS

SERVES 4

3 large red onions

Heaped 2 Tbsp finely chopped fresh flat-leaf parsley

Heaped 2 Tbsp finely chopped fresh cilantro

3 garlic cloves, minced

¾ tsp turmeric

½ tsp ground ginger

Salt and freshly ground black pepper

2 Tbsp olive oil

2¼ lb/1 kg bone-in leg of lamb, cut crosswise into 1¼-in-/3-cm-thick pieces

1 Tbsp sugar

1 tsp ground cinnamon

Finely chop one of the onions. In a tagine, flame-proof casserole, or large, heavy skillet or sauté pan, add the chopped onion, parsley, cilantro, garlic, turmeric, and ginger. Season with salt and pepper and drizzle in the olive oil. Mix well and spread evenly across the bottom of the tagine. Place the lamb pieces snugly together on top.

Cut the remaining two onions into even ⅓-in-/8-mm-thick slices; do not separate the rings. Carefully lay the slices across the top of the lamb. Sprinkle the sugar and cinnamon over the onions. Drizzle ½ cup/120 ml water into the side of the tagine so that it does not rinse the sugar and cinnamon off the onions.

Cover and cook over medium heat for 5 minutes. Reduce the heat to low and cook until the lamb is very tender, 1½ to 2 hours, occasionally nudging the pieces of lamb to keep them from sticking. Dribble in water as necessary to keep the lamb moist, or remove the lid to evaporate and thicken the sauce.

Serve in the tagine. Alternatively, carefully lift out the lamb pieces topped with onion rings, place on plates, and top with the sauce.

In the middle of the twentieth century, La Maison Arabe was the most famous restaurant on the African continent. A French woman and her daughter opened it in 1946, after the pasha Thami el Glaoui granted them the right for the first restaurant in the medina open to foreigners and provided one of his chefs. Frequented by Winston Churchill, Charles de Gaulle, Queen Ingrid of Denmark, and Jackie Kennedy, La Maison Arabe remained a legendary, essential dining spot until the *mesdames* shuttered it in 1983. Fabrizio Ruspoli, an Italian-French aristocrat who spent much time during his childhood in Tanger, purchased the property in 1995 and converted it into Marrakech's first boutique hotel. Over the years, the food has regained its prominent place, and the kitchen is once again the finest in the city.

This sophisticated tagine from the La Maison Arabe kitchen, using the trademark mixing of sweet and savory, and drawing on the citrus groves around Marrakech, is guaranteed to impress. Sublime.

LAMB TAGINE WITH ORANGES, SAFFRON, AND CANDIED ORANGE PEEL

SERVES 4

1 tsp butter, softened

1 tsp ground ginger

½ tsp *ras el hanout* (see page 52)

½ tsp ground cinnamon

½ tsp turmeric

¼ tsp freshly ground white pepper

Generous 1 pinch saffron threads

Salt

2 Tbsp olive oil

2¼ lb/1 kg bone-in leg of lamb, cut into 8 or so pieces

1 small cinnamon stick, broken in half

1 medium red onion, finely chopped

2 Tbsp fresh orange juice

1 tsp honey

1 Valencia orange, scrubbed

¼ cup/50 g sugar

8 cloves

1 tsp toasted sesame seeds for garnishing

CONTINUED

In a tagine, flameproof casserole, or large, heavy skillet or sauté pan, add the butter, ginger, *ras el hanout*, cinnamon, turmeric, white pepper, and saffron. Season with salt. Moisten with the olive oil and blend well. One by one, place the pieces of lamb in the spice mixture, and turn to coat. Add half of the cinnamon stick and scatter the onion across the top.

Place the tagine over medium heat, cover, and cook, turning the lamb from time to time, until the meat is browned and the onion is softened but not scorched, about 15 minutes. Add 1 cup/240 ml water, loosely cover, and cook over medium-low heat for 45 minutes, stirring from time to time. Add ½ cup/120 ml water and 1 Tbsp of the orange juice and cook until the meat is tender, about 45 minutes. Add a bit more water if necessary to keep the sauce loose, or remove the lid to evaporate and thicken it. Stir in the honey and cook the lamb uncovered for a final 5 minutes.

Meanwhile, peel the orange, reserving the fruit. With a knife, scrape away some—but not all—of the white pith from the peel. Cut the peel into long, very thin strips about ⅛ in/3 mm wide.

In a small pan, bring ½ cup/120 ml water to a boil. Add the strips of peel and a pinch of salt, and simmer for 2 minutes. Drain, discard the liquid, and rinse out the pan. Return the strips to the pan, cover with ¾ cup/180 ml water, and bring to a boil. Stir in the sugar and add the remaining cinnamon stick and the cloves. Simmer until the liquid is syrupy and the strips of peel are tender but still a touch al dente, about 20 minutes. Stir in the remaining 1 Tbsp orange juice, remove from the heat, and let cool.

With a sharp knife, cut away any white pith from the reserved orange. Carefully cut along the membranes separating the segments and remove them. Lay the segments in a shallow bowl, spoon the syrup from the pan over the segments, and let soak until ready to serve.

To serve, divide the lamb among four plates, and top with the sauce, orange segments, and strips of caramelized peel. Lightly sprinkle with the sesame seeds.

This is an emblematic dish of Eid al-Adha, one of the most important feasts of the year. To commemorate Abraham's willingness to sacrifice his son, lambs are slaughtered and prepared across the country. It remains a fundamental dish—and one of Morocco's most dazzling. At the end of cooking, the sauce should be a thick, deep brown glaze. *Ras el hanout* is key, giving spicy background notes to the honeyed sweetness.

SALTY-SWEET
GLAZED LAMB WITH ALMONDS AND RAISINS

m'rouzia

SERVES 6

1 Tbsp *ras el hanout* (see page 52)

1 tsp ground ginger

½ tsp ground mace

1 pinch saffron threads, dry-toasted and ground (see page 50)

1 tsp sea salt

½ tsp freshly ground black pepper

¼ cup/60 ml olive oil

4 lb/1.8 kg bone-in lamb leg, shoulder, or saddle, cut into 10 or so thick pieces

2 Tbsp butter, cut into pieces

2 medium red onions, chopped

About 1½ cups/225 g raisins

1 tsp ground cinnamon

½ cup/120 ml honey

¾ cup/115 g unsalted toasted almonds without skins

In a large, heavy pot, Dutch oven, or flameproof casserole, add the *ras el hanout*, ginger, mace, saffron, salt, and pepper. Moisten with the olive oil and blend well. One by one, place the pieces of lamb into the mixture and turn to coat. Add the butter and scatter the onions across the top.

Place the pot over medium heat, cover, and cook the lamb, turning from time to time, until browned and fragrant, 8 to 10 minutes. Add 2 cups/480 ml water, loosely cover, and cook over low heat for 1¼ hours. Add a bit of water if needed to keep the sauce loose.

Add the raisins, cinnamon, and honey. Cook uncovered until the sauce has reduced to a rich glaze, 1 to 1½ hours. The meat should come easily away from the bone.

In a small skillet, warm the almonds over medium-low heat until fragrant, about 2 minutes.

To serve, arrange the pieces of meat on a serving platter, cover with any remaining glaze in the pan, and top with the warmed almonds.

This potent, super-savory lamb dish is typical in Salé, a walled medieval city just across the mouth of the Bou Regreg River from Rabat. Generous chunks of lamb or kid are rubbed in a salty garlic paste and ground cumin, and cooked until nearly falling off the bone. Then—and this is what makes the dish stand out—ground coriander seeds and olive oil are added to the pot, and the sauce is reduced until it is thick and dark, bold and a bit salty. The recipe comes from Meriem Kherchouf, the mother of a good friend in Rabat, who insists on serving the meat with a pot of Mint Tea. The tea aids digestion and adds to the perfect combination of flavors. Serve with plenty of bread.

The lamb is even better the next day, pulled from the bone and stuffed into pockets of bread for sandwiches.

LAMB WITH GARLIC, CUMIN, AND CORIANDER

mkila

SERVES 6

3½ lb/1.6 kg bone-in leg of lamb or kid, cut into 8 or 10 pieces
10 medium garlic cloves
1 Tbsp sea salt
2 Tbsp ground cumin
⅓ cup/75 ml olive oil
2 Tbsp ground coriander
Mint Tea (page 210)

Rinse the lamb and place in a large mixing bowl.

In a mortar, pound the garlic with the salt into a smooth paste. Rub over the pieces of lamb. Sprinkle with 1 Tbsp of the cumin and rub into the lamb. Turn the pieces, sprinkle with the remaining 1 Tbsp cumin, and rub in.

Transfer to a large, heavy pot, Dutch oven, or flameproof casserole with a snug-fitting lid. Pour 2½ cups/600 ml water into the mixing bowl, swirl to pick up any remaining spices, and pour into the pot.

Cover and cook over medium-low heat until the meat is very tender and comes away easily from the bone, about 1½ hours, moving the meat from time to time to keep it from sticking. Add a bit of water if needed to keep the sauce loose.

Add the olive oil and ground coriander and cook uncovered over medium heat until the liquid has evaporated and the sauce is thick and dark, about 20 minutes.

Place the meat on a serving dish or in a tagine, and cover with the sauce. Serve with the Mint Tea.

Pulling away pieces of succulent roast lamb and dipping them into cumin and salt is one of Morocco's great culinary treats. In the home kitchen, it is very difficult to spit-roast a whole lamb, as is done for large Moroccan celebrations. A delicious version can be prepared by steaming a shoulder or leg of lamb in a large pot until the meat falls off the bone, seasoning it with cumin, then roasting the meat in the oven to give it a golden crust. It's a straightforward method that yields festive results.

Serve with a platter of steamed seasonal vegetables or oven-baked potatoes.

ROAST LAMB with CUMIN

mechoui

SERVES 4 TO 6

One 4¼-lb/2-kg bone-in lamb shoulder or leg of lamb
Coarse sea salt
2 Tbsp butter or *smen* (see page 45)
Ground cumin for rubbing and dipping

Fill a large pot fitted with a steamer basket or a couscoussier with water to just below the steamer basket.

Cut the lamb through the bone, but no further, in order to fit it into the steamer basket. Rub the lamb with salt and place in the basket. Cover and steam until the meat is very tender and falling off the bone, 1¼ to 1½ hours. Check occasionally to make sure that the pot has enough water and doesn't go dry.

Preheat the oven to 400°F/200°C/gas mark 6.

Transfer the lamb to a roasting pan. Rub with the butter and a generous amount of cumin and salt. Roast until deeply golden, about 20 minutes, turning after about 10 minutes. The meat should come away easily with a fork.

Serve on a platter along with individual small dishes of cumin and salt for dipping the lamb.

In the Rif Mountains, Berbers raise goats to make delicious fresh cheeses from their milk and stew their meat in unglazed tagines. This succulent tagine, with its ideal blending of flavors, has its inspiration in a unforgettable winter lunch in the Rif during a trip to hunt wild mushrooms. Either of the common types of dried figs will work here—the stacked flat golden ones or the darker, pear-shaped variety. The flat ones are the first choice. There is no need to soak the figs in advance.

KID TAGINE
WITH DRIED
FIGS AND THYME

SERVES 4

3 unpeeled garlic cloves

Heaped 3 Tbsp finely chopped fresh flat-leaf parsley

1 tsp dried oregano or *zaâtar* (see page 48)

½ tsp ground ginger

½ tsp turmeric

Salt and freshly ground black pepper

5 Tbsp/75 ml olive oil

Two 1-lb/455-g kid legs, each cut crosswise into 3 pieces

2 medium red onions, roughly chopped

About 16 dried flat golden figs

2 sprigs fresh thyme

Toasted sesame seeds for garnishing

Peel and mince one of the garlic cloves. In a large mixing bowl, add the minced garlic, parsley, oregano, ginger, and turmeric. Season with salt and pepper. Moisten with the olive oil and blend well. Place each piece of the kid in the marinade and turn to coat. Spread the onions over the kid. Cover and marinate for 1 hour, turning from time to time.

In a tagine, flameproof casserole, or large, heavy skillet or sauté pan, put the meat and onions and any remaining marinade. Place the tagine over medium heat, loosely cover, and cook the meat, turning the pieces from time to time, until browned, about 10 minutes.

Place the figs over and around the kid and top with the thyme. Gently crush the remaining two unpeeled garlic cloves under the heel of your palm or the side of a heavy knife. Add to the tagine. Drizzle 1 cup/240 ml water into the side of the tagine and loosely cover. Reduce the heat to low and cook until the meat is tender, 1¼ to 1½ hours, turning the pieces occasionally. Add a bit more water if necessary to keep the sauce loose, or remove the lid to evaporate and thicken it.

Sprinkle a pinch of sesame seeds over the figs and serve.

This classic tagine is a glorious blend of sweet and savory. Stewed in a sauce spiced with ginger, nutmeg, cinnamon, and turmeric, the succulent pieces of meat are served topped with caramelized apricots and jewel-like prunes rolled in toasted sesame seeds plus a scattering of crunchy fried almonds.

Sanae Nouali, the cook from Larache (between Rabat and Tanger) whose recipe I have adapted here, only uses the most tender cut of meat, the front shank that is low on the leg and farthest from the shoulder.

SWEET
VEAL SHANK TAGINE
WITH CARAMELIZED
PRUNES AND APRICOTS

SERVES 4 TO 6

2 medium red onions, 1 grated and 1 chopped

1 Tbsp ground ginger

½ tsp turmeric

½ tsp ground nutmeg

1 tsp ground cinnamon

Heaped 2 Tbsp finely chopped fresh flat-leaf parsley

Salt and freshly ground black pepper

½ cup/120 ml olive oil

3 lb/1.4 kg bone-in center-cut veal shanks, cut into 12 or so pieces

1 cup/170 g prunes with pits (see Note)

1 cup/170 g dried apricots

2 Tbsp sugar

2 Tbsp butter

Orange flower water

1 cup/240 ml light olive oil or vegetable oil for frying

½ cup/60 g raw almonds, blanched and skins removed (see page 41)

⅓ cup/45 g toasted sesame seeds

In a large mixing bowl, add the grated onion, ginger, turmeric, nutmeg, ½ tsp of the cinnamon, and the parsley. Season with salt and pepper. Moisten with the ½ cup/120 ml olive oil and blend well. Place the meat piece by piece in the marinade, and turn to coat. Cover and marinate for 1 hour, turning from time to time.

In a tagine, flameproof casserole, or large, heavy skillet or sauté pan, put the meat and any remaining marinade. Cover with the chopped onion. Place the tagine over medium heat and cook, turning the pieces from time to time, until browned, 10 to 15 minutes.

Stir in 1 cup/240 ml water, loosely cover, and cook over medium heat, stirring from time to time, for 1 hour. Add ½ cup/120 ml water, and cook over low heat until the meat is tender, about 30 minutes. There should be about 1 cup/240 ml of sauce at the end. Add more water if necessary to keep the sauce loose, or remove the lid to evaporate and thicken it.

Meanwhile, in a saucepan, place the prunes and apricots, sprinkle with the sugar and remaining ½ tsp cinnamon. Add the butter, a few drops of orange flower water, and 1½ cups/360 ml water. Bring to a boil, reduce the heat to medium, and cook uncovered at a gentle boil until the liquid is syrupy, 20 to 30 minutes. Remove from the heat and let cool.

In a small saucepan, heat the 1 cup/240 ml oil over medium-high heat. Add the almonds and fry, stirring to cook evenly, until golden, 1 to 2 minutes. Transfer with a slotted spoon to paper towels to drain.

To serve, arrange the veal on a large serving platter. Spoon the sauce of the top. Put the sesame seeds in a small mixing bowl. Roll each prune in the sesame seeds and carefully place on the veal. Arrange the apricots around the edges of the meat and scatter the fried almonds over the top.

NOTE: *Prunes with pits retain their shape and texture, while pitted ones collapse. If using pitted prunes, cook them for 10 minutes, adding them to the boiling liquid with the apricots toward the end.*

The pronounced contrasts between the sweet and savory here are delightful. The sweet pears remain somewhat "fresh" with a background of spice (ginger, clove, cinnamon), while offering a contrast to the lusty, savory flavors of the meat. The peeled pear halves, each studded with a clove, look dazzling on top of the braised pieces of meat.

VEAL SHANK TAGINE WITH PEARS

SERVES 4 TO 6

2 medium red onions, thinly sliced

1 tsp ground ginger

½ tsp turmeric

½ tsp freshly ground black pepper

1 pinch saffron threads, dry-toasted and ground (see page 50)

Salt

¼ cup/60 ml olive oil

3 lb/1.4 kg bone-in center-cut veal shanks, cut into 12 or so pieces

1 small cinnamon stick

FOR THE PEARS

3 or 4 very firm pears, such as Conference, Anjou, or Williams

8 to 10 cloves

2 pinches ground cinnamon

2 pinches ground ginger

About 1 cup plus 2 Tbsp/225 g superfine sugar

½ tsp orange flower water

In a tagine, flameproof casserole, or large, heavy skillet or sauté pan, add the onions, ginger, turmeric, pepper, and saffron. Season with salt. Moisten with the olive oil and blend well. Add the meat and turn to coat.

Cook over medium heat, stirring from time to time, for 15 minutes until the meat has browned but without scorching the onions. Add the cinnamon stick and 1 cup/240 ml water, and cook over medium-low heat, stirring from time to time, for 1 hour. Add ½ cup/120 ml water and cook over low heat until the meat is tender, about 30 minutes. Add a bit more water if necessary to keep the sauce loose, or remove the lid to evaporate and thicken it.

MEANWHILE, PREPARE THE PEARS. Peel, halve, and core the pears. Pierce the outside of each half with 1 clove. In a large skillet or sauté pan, place the pears, remaining cloves, ground cinnamon, and ginger. Cover with 2 cups/480 ml cold water. Simmer uncovered over medium heat for 25 minutes, gently turning the pears from time to time. Stir in the sugar and cook for 15 minutes until the liquid is syrupy, basting the pears as needed. Sprinkle in the orange flower water. Remove from the heat and cover until ready to use.

To serve, place the meat on a platter or individual plates, spoon the sauce over the top, and arrange the pears over the meat. Drizzle with some of the syrupy sauce.

The southern outpost of Fort Bou-Jerif is set in a scrub-filled landscape of dried river-beds and boulders, home to an array of animals—jackals and foxes, gazelles, lizards and turtles, scorpions—and to an old French Foreign Legion fort that lies in ruins nearby. A slow drive down the frequently washed-out *piste* (track) leads to Guelmim, with its famed, centuries-running Saturday market whose livestock section is dominated by the dromedary, or camel, the region's main meat. Cooking over an ember-filled brazier in the outpost's restaurant kitchen, Ali Amrou, a young Berber cook, prepares this tagine with camel as well as with beef or veal. It is a straightforward tagine, almost frugal, even in its spicing, but it is hearty and draws on seasonal ingredients for topping the meat. If desired, substitute green beans for the peas. See Chicken Tagine with French Green Beans (page 143) for preparing the beans.

VEAL SHANK TAGINE
with PEAS

SERVES 4

2½ Tbsp olive oil

2¼ lb/1 kg bone-in center-cut veal shanks,
    cut into 4 to 6 pieces

2 medium red onions, chopped

3 ripe medium tomatoes, seeded and chopped

1 Tbsp finely chopped fresh flat-leaf parsley

1 Tbsp finely chopped fresh cilantro

1 tsp sweet paprika

½ tsp ground cumin

½ tsp turmeric

1 pinch ground cinnamon

Salt and freshly ground black pepper

1 cup/140 g shucked peas or frozen petit pois

In a tagine, flameproof casserole, or large, heavy skillet or sauté pan, add the olive oil and swirl to coat the bottom. Place the meat on top. Cover and cook over medium heat for 10 minutes, turning from time to time.

Add the onions and cook for 5 minutes, turning the pieces of meat a couple times. Add the tomatoes, parsley, cilantro, paprika, cumin, turmeric, and cinnamon. Season with salt and pepper. Cover snugly and cook over medium-low heat for about 45 minutes, turning the pieces of meat from time to time and making sure the tagine does not dry out. Add ¾ cup/ 180 ml water, loosely cover, and cook over low heat until the meat is tender and comes easily away from the bone, 45 to 60 minutes.

Meanwhile, in a small saucepan, boil the peas in lightly salted water until tender but not mushy, about 5 minutes. Drain.

Scatter the peas across the top of the meat, loosely cover, and cook for a final 5 minutes before serving.

This popular, homey dish of small meatballs stewed in tomato sauce often has a particularly delicious touch—making space between the meatballs, cracking in eggs, and cooking them in the sauce. Another option is to fry the eggs in a skillet and then place them on top of individual servings of the meatballs. This tagine is a great winter dish, as it uses canned tomatoes.

KEFTA MEATBALL TAGINE
IN TOMATO SAUCE
WITH EGGS

SERVES 4

1¼ lb/570 g ground beef
½ medium red onion, grated
2 garlic cloves, minced
½ tsp ground cumin
½ tsp sweet paprika
½ tsp ground cinnamon
Heaped 1 Tbsp finely chopped fresh flat-leaf parsley
Heaped 1 Tbsp finely chopped fresh cilantro
Salt and freshly ground black pepper
1½ cups/250 g canned peeled whole Italian plum tomatoes, seeded, with juice
2 Tbsp olive oil
4 large eggs

In a mixing bowl, add the meat, onion, one of the garlic cloves, and ¼ tsp each of the cumin, paprika, cinnamon, parsley, and cilantro. Season with salt and pepper and blend into a consistent, smooth paste. Taking spoonfuls of the mix, roll meatballs that are about 1¼ in/3 cm in diameter. There should be about 36 total.

In a food processor, using quick pulses, purée the tomatoes and their juice.

In a tagine, flameproof casserole, or large, heavy skillet or sauté pan, add the olive oil and tomatoes, season with salt, and cook over medium-low heat until deep red and thicker, about 15 minutes. Stir in the remaining garlic, spices, and herbs.

Gently set the meatballs in the tomato sauce. Cook uncovered for 5 minutes, gently turning the meatballs with a pair of spoons until browned on all sides. Dribble in ¼ cup/60 ml water, loosely cover, and cook over low heat for 40 minutes. The tomato sauce should be a little loose. Add a bit more water if necessary to keep the sauce loose, or remove the lid to evaporate and thicken it.

Make four spaces between the meatballs and gently crack the eggs into the tagine. Cover and cook until the eggs set, about 5 minutes. Serve immediately.

Like the tagine, the *tangia* is named for the terra-cotta pot in which it is cooked—in this case, an elongated, double-handled crock (see page 55). Filled with chunks of beef, veal, or lamb; seasoned with spices, garlic, and preserved lemon; and sealed with heavy brown butcher paper secured with string, the pot cooks slowly for hours until the meat is succulent and the sauce rich.

This classic *tangia*—with just meat and spices, no vegetables or legumes—is considered something of a man's dish, as, on Fridays, it was common to drop the pot at the *hammam* (steam bath) and pick it up later, once the dish had cooked for a number of hours in the ashes. A *tangia* can be prepared at home in a heavy, upright (as opposed to wide) pot, a Dutch oven, a pressure cooker, or even a bean crock, and cooked in the oven or on the stove top, the method in this recipe. Thick, cross-cut veal shanks with the bone are perfect here, with the marrow adding an unctuousness to the rich, fragrant sauce. Serve with a selection of steamed seasonal vegetables as well as bread.

MARRAKECH TANGIA

tangia

SERVES 4 TO 6

8 garlic cloves, lightly crushed

½ preserved lemon (see page 45), quartered, seeded, and finely chopped

1 tsp ground ginger

1 tsp ground cumin

½ tsp turmeric

Generous 1 pinch saffron threads, dry-toasted and ground (see page 50)

2 Tbsp butter or *smen* (see page 45)

3 Tbsp olive oil

Salt and freshly ground black pepper

3½ lb/1.6 kg bone-in center-cut veal or lamb shanks, cut into 8 to 10 thick pieces

1 small bouquet fresh cilantro, tied

In a large mixing bowl, add the garlic, preserved lemon, ginger, cumin, turmeric, saffron, butter, and olive oil. Season with salt and pepper. Add the meat and turn to coat.

In a heavy pot, Dutch oven, bean crock with a tight-fitting lid, or tangia, add the meat and spice mixture as well as the cilantro. Pour 1¾ cups/420 ml water into the mixing bowl, swirl to pick up any remaining spices, and add to the pot. Cover the pot tightly and cook over medium heat for 15 minutes. Reduce the heat to its lowest possible level, and cook covered until the meat comes easily off the bone, about 2½ hours. Loosen the lid at the end to evaporate and thicken the sauce.

Transfer the meat and sauce to a platter. Remove and discard the cilantro. Serve immediately.

EGGS AND POULTRY

Strolling through small villages in rural Morocco, it's common to see chickens—brilliantly plumed copper brown birds with black tails and red combs—pecking around the ocher-red earth for stray seeds and insects. From the kitchens in such small towns to the center of the largest cities, chicken is a key ingredient and stars in some of the country's most famous dishes. Chicken Tagine with Preserved Lemons and Olives (page 140) is one of those. Chicken in Buttery Saffron-Onion Sauce with Almonds (see page 147), a specialty of Fès, is another. Today, a number of dishes once made almost exclusively with lamb—say, a tagine topped by a caramelized compote of tomatoes (see page 144)—are commonly done with chicken. Less expensive, perhaps, chicken is also able to absorb, and show off, the spicing of the sauces.

Turkeys, too, can be seen poking around in some villages in the Berber Atlas, quail and pigeon find their way into a handful of special dishes, and in the palm oases, cooks stuff young pigeon and stew them in tagines (see page 137).

Eggs also appear in tagines. In the coastal city of Essaouira, whisked egg is poured over and around a saucy braised chicken and cooked until just set (see page 148). Especially in the southern Atlas ranges, eggs can be the protagonists in tagines. These simple dishes, with onions, tomatoes, and peppers, a few olives, and some cumin and fresh cilantro (see facing page), are, like much of the cuisine of this region, hearty and filling.

See page 55 for more information on cooking with tagines.

On the eastern side of the High Atlas and through the Drâa Valley in the Anti-Atlas, simple egg tagines often replace meat ones. Essentially, vegetables are cooked in the tagine and then the eggs are poured over the top, seasoned (cumin and cilantro are key), covered with the conical lid, and left to cook until set. This type of simple, delicious tagine is called an *omelette berbère*.

One or two yolks are left whole and are cooked away from the center of the tagine so that they stay runny. The yolks are then broken with bread when the omelet is eaten.

BERBER OMELET TAGINE

SERVES 4

1 medium red onion, finely chopped

1 Italian green pepper or ½ green bell pepper, seeded, deribbed, and finely chopped

Salt and freshly ground black pepper

3 Tbsp olive oil

1 garlic clove, minced

2 ripe medium tomatoes, seeded and finely chopped

8 large eggs

Heaped 2 to 3 Tbsp finely chopped fresh cilantro

Generous 2 or 3 pinches ground cumin

16 black or green olives with pits, rinsed

In a tagine, flameproof casserole, or large, heavy skillet or sauté pan, put the onion and green pepper. Season with salt and pepper.

Moisten with the olive oil and swirl to coat the vegetables. Cook uncovered over medium heat until the vegetables are soft and fragrant, about 10 minutes. Add the garlic and cook for 1 minute. Add the tomatoes and 2 Tbsp water and cook, stirring from time to time, until the tomatoes have softened, about 8 minutes.

In a bowl, whisk six of the eggs until spongy. Add the remaining two eggs and loosely stir in without breaking the yolks.

Pour the eggs into the pan, carefully moving the two yolks away from the center. Sprinkle with the cilantro and cumin, and place the olives around the pan. Cover, turn the heat to the lowest possible setting, and cook without stirring until the eggs are set but still moist, about 15 minutes. Serve in the tagine.

After a soggy winter's morning hunting mushrooms in the cork- and pine-covered Rif Mountains with a couple of local guides, my family and I returned to a rural lodge called Auberge Dardara with owner Jaber El Hababi. Our wicker baskets brimmed with three of the three dozen varieties of edible wild mushrooms found in the nearby hills: chanterelles, meaty cèpes (porcini) with yellow-tinted undercaps, and a type of coral Ramaria the size of cauliflower and the color of wet hay. We happily passed our spoils to the chef.

After cleaning and slicing the mushrooms, he sautéed them hot and fast to sear in the juices, as flames shot up from the blackened skillet in the smoky kitchen. He whisked some eggs, seasoned them with healthy pinches of local herbs, and prepared a pair of divine omelets. A just reward for the drizzly hunt!

As the omelets need to be individually cooked, instructions below are given for a single wide, thin omelet. If preparing more than one, sauté the mushrooms by variety but cook the omelets individually.

RIF MOUNTAIN OMELET WITH WILD MUSHROOMS

MAKES ONE 8-IN/20-CM OMELET; SERVES 1 OR 2

½ lb/225 g wild mushrooms of at least 2 or
   3 varieties
3 or 4 Tbsp extra-virgin olive oil, plus more
   for drizzling
Salt and freshly ground black pepper
3 large eggs
1 tsp dried oregano or *zaâtar* (see page 48),
   plus more for garnishing
1 unpeeled garlic clove
1 Tbsp finely chopped fresh flat-leaf parsley,
   plus more for garnishing
1 dried bay leaf

Keeping the mushroom varieties separate, brush them clean. Fill a bowl with water. Quickly dunk the mushrooms in a few changes of water just before cooking. Drain and pat dry with paper towels. Quarter or slice the mushrooms depending on their shape.

In a 10-in/25-cm skillet, heat 1 Tbsp of the olive oil until smoking. Add one mushroom variety, season with a pinch of salt and pepper, and quickly sauté until the edges are golden, 1 to 2 minutes. Transfer to a plate. Add another 1 Tbsp olive oil to the pan and sauté the second mushroom variety. Repeat if needed for a third variety.

In a small bowl, whisk the eggs until spongy. Stir in the 1 tsp oregano and a pinch of salt. Add three-fourths of the mushrooms and turn to coat. Gently crush the garlic under the heel of your palm or the side of a heavy knife.

CONTINUED

Add 1 Tbsp olive oil and the garlic to the pan and cook over medium heat until fragrant, about 1 minute. Remove the garlic and reserve.

Pour the egg mixture into the pan. Immediately swirl the pan for a few seconds to keep the mixture from sticking as the eggs begin to set. Sprinkle the 1 Tbsp parsley over the top and season with salt and pepper. Place the bay leaf in the center. Cover, reduce the heat to medium-low, and cook until the bottom is golden and the omelet is set but still moist, 2 to 3 minutes. Do not turn or stir the eggs; only swirl the pan from time to time to keep the omelet from sticking.

Loosen the omelet with a thin spatula if necessary and slide onto a large, flat plate. Scatter the remaining mushrooms over the top along with a pinch of parsley and some oregano. Top with the reserved garlic clove, drizzle with olive oil, and serve immediately.

The city of Ouarzazate lies between the High Atlas and the Anti-Atlas at an important crossroads of a couple different valleys. Extending from the east side of the city is its vast and productive *palmeraie* (date palm grove). The kitchen of Dar Daïf, a family-run hotel on the edge of the *palmeraie* whose cooking many consider to be the best in the region, draws on seasonal, local products from the grove, including pigeons. Most spectacularly, the cooks stuff squabs (young pigeons) with an aromatic date and almond paste and serve them with steamed and sweetened vermicelli pasta. It's a sensational combination.

Stewing squab can be challenging. They are difficult to find fresh. Their thin, delicate skin tears easily, and their dark, strong meat needs extended cooking. Poussin—a young chicken weighing around 1 lb/455 g—makes an ideal substitution in this recipe adapted from Dar Daïf. The skin is far less delicate, and because a poussin is slightly more fatty, the meat stays moister while stewing. Poussin meat is paler and finer than squab, requires less cooking time, and has a smoother flavor, and therefore is better able to absorb the rich, complex spicing of the sauce and stuffing.

The stuffing is sweet and aromatic, as is the sauce. To give the sauce more bite, add a couple of pinches of *ras el hanout* (see page 52). Sweet Couscous (page 205) may be served with the poussin in place of the Sweet Vermicelli.

DATE-AND-ALMOND-STUFFED POUSSINS WITH SWEET VERMICELLI

SERVES 4

10 *mejhoul* dates or other large, sweet dates, pitted
¾ cup/100 g ground almonds
2 tsp rose water or orange flower water
⅛ tsp ground cinnamon
Four 1-lb/455-g poussins
3 Tbsp olive oil
2 medium red onions, chopped
Heaped 2 Tbsp finely chopped fresh cilantro
1½ tsp ground ginger

4 cloves
1 pinch saffron threads, dry-toasted and ground (see page 50)
¼ tsp white pepper
1 small cinnamon stick or 2 small pieces cinnamon bark
Salt
Sweet Vermicelli (recipe follows)

CONTINUED

In a saucepan fitted with a steamer basket, steam six of the dates for 5 minutes to soften. Reserve the remaining four dates for garnishing. In a small mixing bowl, mash the steamed dates with the ground almonds, rose water, and cinnamon into a smooth paste.

Rinse the outside of the poussins as well as the cavities, being careful not to tear the skins. Using about half of the paste, stuff each bird with about 3 Tbsp. (There will be leftover paste.) Securely tie the legs of each bird with cotton kitchen string.

In a tagine, flameproof casserole, or heavy pot, add the olive oil and onions and cook over medium heat until the onions begin to turn translucent, about 8 minutes. Place the birds breast-side up in the tagine and cook for 2 minutes. Turn breast-side down and cook for another 2 minutes. Sprinkle the cilantro, ginger, cloves, saffron, and white pepper around the birds. Add the cinnamon stick, season with salt, and drizzle in 2 cups/480 ml water. Loosely cover and cook over medium heat for 40 minutes. Gently turn the birds breast-side up and cook uncovered until done—a leg jiggled lightly should feel loose—and the sauce is reduced, 20 to 30 minutes. There should be about 1 cup/240 ml of sauce at the end.

Make an incision across the top of the remaining four dates and stuff with the remaining almond paste. The paste should bulge slightly from the openings in the dates. Make an attractive hash-mark pattern in the paste with a knife.

Place the stuffed dates around the birds and serve with the vermicelli on the side. Alternatively, divide the birds among four plates, spoon the sauce on top, and place a stuffed date beside each bird.

Traditionally, the short noodles are steamed several times in a couscoussier, as for couscous. Unlike couscous, vermicelli is covered while it steams. This unusual method is the one used here. Although the final texture of the noodles will be slightly less "dry" than if steaming, there is a much quicker way to prepare the vermicelli. Boil the noodles in lightly salted water until al dente (a couple of minutes at most), drain, quickly rinse with water to stop further cooking, and then toss with olive oil to prevent sticking or clumping.

SWEET VERMICELLI

shariya seffa

SERVES 4

Salt
10 oz/280 g vermicelli or angel hair pasta, broken into 1-in/2.5-cm pieces
2 Tbsp olive oil
1 Tbsp butter, softened

Powdered sugar for dusting
¼ cup/30 g chopped unsalted toasted almonds
Ground cinnamon for dusting

Fill the bottom of a couscoussier or a large pot with a steamer basket with 3 or 4 in/7.5 or 10 cm of water or enough to reach just below the basket. Bring to a boil and add a generous pinch of salt. Place a strip of aluminum foil or plastic wrap around the rim, and place the steamer basket snugly on top.

In a very wide, shallow dish or *gsâa*, add the vermicelli, drizzle with the olive oil, and stir until evenly coated with olive oil. Transfer to the basket for the first steaming. Cover and steam for 10 minutes.

Dump the pasta into the dish, breaking it up and spreading it around with a wooden spoon. Sprinkle with ½ cup/120 ml of cool water, season with salt, stir, and let sit for 5 minutes to absorb the water. Toss with your hands.

Transfer the pasta to the basket for a second steaming. Cover and steam for 5 minutes.

Dump the pasta into the dish again, breaking it up and spreading it around with the wooden spoon. Sprinkle with ½ cup/120 ml of cool water, stir, and let sit for 5 minutes to absorb the water. Toss with your hands.

Transfer the pasta to the basket for a third steaming. Cover and steam for 5 minutes.

Once again, dump the pasta into the dish, breaking it up and spreading it around with the wooden spoon. Taste the pasta. It should be tender and a touch al dente. If not, add a small amount of cool water, let the pasta absorb it, and then steam a fourth, or even a fifth, time.

When the pasta is done, add the butter, generously dust with powdered sugar, and toss. In a serving bowl, gently mound the pasta, place the almonds on the crown, and make decorative stripes of ground cinnamon running down the sides.

This is one of the country's most famous dishes, and any book on Moroccan cuisine or trip to the country would be incomplete without it. I have eaten this unique blending of disparate flavors for lunch or dinner in a number of different homes, but it is considered something of a special dish, offered at celebrations including weddings.

The dish is usually served with a tall stack of freshly baked bread. I had it once, though, very memorably, prepared in Marrakech by Khadija Dilali (see her divine Black Olive, Walnut, and Onion Bread, page 66) with white rice and yogurt-mint sauce on the side. The soothing, smooth flavors complemented the bold, savory, and tart ones of the tagine to perfection.

This recipe uses a whole chicken, but can be as easily prepared with bone-in chicken breasts, thighs, or legs, or a mixture of them.

CHICKEN TAGINE
WITH
PRESERVED LEMONS
AND OLIVES

SERVES 4

FOR THE RICE
1½ cups/300 g white rice
Salt
1 Tbsp butter, softened

FOR THE YOGURT SAUCE
1 cup/240 ml thick plain yogurt
3 Tbsp milk
Salt
1 Tbsp finely chopped fresh mint or 1 tsp
    dried mint

One 4¼-lb/1.9-kg chicken
1 preserved lemon (see page 45)
2 garlic cloves, minced

3 Tbsp finely chopped fresh flat-leaf parsley
3 Tbsp finely chopped fresh cilantro
1 tsp ground ginger
½ tsp turmeric
Generous 1 pinch saffron threads, dry-toasted
    and ground (see page 50)
Salt and freshly ground white pepper
2 Tbsp olive oil
2 Tbsp fresh lemon juice
2 medium red onions, finely chopped
1 Tbsp butter or *smen* (see page 45)
1 cup/170 g green or violet olives with pits

CONTINUED

PREPARE THE RICE. In a large saucepan, boil the rice in lightly salted water until just tender, 12 to 20 minutes, depending on the rice. Pour into a strainer, quickly rinse with hot water, and rinse out the saucepan. Return the rice to the saucepan, add the butter, stir well, and set aside until ready to serve.

PREPARE THE YOGURT SAUCE. In a small bowl, whisk together the yogurt and milk with a pinch of salt and the mint. It should be just thin enough to dribble off a spoon; add another 1 Tbsp or so of milk if needed. Cover and refrigerate until ready to serve.

Clip off the chicken wing tips and the fatty "tail," and trim any excess fat that can be reached without tearing the skin. Rinse the outside of the chicken and the cavity, and pat dry with paper towels.

Quarter the preserved lemon lengthwise, rinse, and remove the seeds. Without breaking the peel, scrape away the pulp with a spoon; reserve the peel. Finely chop the pulp.

In a small mixing bowl, add the lemon pulp and any juices, garlic, parsley, cilantro, ginger, turmeric, and saffron. Season with salt and white pepper. Moisten with the olive oil, lemon juice, and 2 Tbsp water and blend well.

Set the chicken in a tagine or a large pot that will comfortably hold the whole chicken. Rub the chicken with the saffron mixture, pushing some of it gently under the edges of the skin.

Place the chicken breast-side up and spoon on the remaining saffron mixture. Tie the feet with cotton kitchen string. Surround the chicken with the onions, add the butter, and drizzle in 1 cup/240 ml water.

Cover and cook over medium heat for 20 minutes. Turn the chicken breast-side down, cover, reduce the heat to low, and cook for 20 minutes. Add 1 cup/240 ml water, loosely cover, and cook until the chicken is very tender, about 50 minutes. Stir in a bit of water if necessary to keep the sauce loose.

Trim two of the preserved lemon peel quarters into attractive shapes, such as leaves with serrated edges or flowers. (The remaining two can either be also trimmed and used, or discarded.)

Preheat the oven to 350°F/180°C/gas mark 4.

Transfer the chicken to a platter to drain for a few minutes. Return the juices to the tagine. Rub the chicken with the remaining ½ Tbsp butter. Place the chicken on a baking sheet and bake until the skin is golden and slightly crispy, 5 to 10 minutes.

Meanwhile, add the olives to the sauce in the tagine and cook, uncovered, over medium-high heat until the sauce has thickened slightly and is no longer watery.

Transfer the chicken to a serving dish breast-side up. Lay the cut lemon peels across the breast. Spoon the sauce and olives around the chicken. Serve with the rice in one bowl and the yogurt sauce in another on the side.

This simple, delightful tagine tops flavorful chicken with slender green beans that still have a slight crispness. The beans are first boiled and then are added to the tagine and cooked for the final 10 minutes. In Morocco, the lengthy season for green beans peaks in the summer months, making this a perfect recipe for a late, lazy lunch or dinner. You can steam the green beans instead of boiling them.

CHICKEN TAGINE
WITH
FRENCH GREEN BEANS

SERVES 4

4 whole chicken legs, split into drumsticks and thighs

2 medium red onions, thinly sliced

3 garlic cloves, minced

Heaped 1 Tbsp finely chopped fresh flat-leaf parsley

Heaped 1 Tbsp finely chopped fresh cilantro

1 tsp ground ginger

1 pinch saffron threads, dry-toasted and ground (see page 50)

Salt and freshly ground white pepper

¼ cup/60 ml olive oil

3 ripe medium tomatoes, halved, seeded, and grated (see Note, page 78)

1 lb/455 g haricots verts, trimmed and cut into 1½-in/4-cm lengths

Toasted sesame seeds for garnishing

Rinse the chicken, remove the skin, and trim any excess fat.

In a large mixing bowl, add the onions, garlic, parsley, cilantro, ginger, and saffron. Season with salt and white pepper. Moisten with the olive oil and blend well. Add the chicken pieces and turn to coat. Cover and marinate for 30 minutes.

In a tagine, flameproof casserole, or large, heavy skillet or sauté pan, add the chicken and all the marinade. Cover and cook over medium heat until the chicken is browned, about 12 minutes, turning the pieces from time to time. Add the tomatoes and ½ cup/120 ml water, loosely cover, and cook over medium-low heat, moving the chicken from time to time to keep it from sticking, until done but not falling off the bone, about 45 minutes. Stir in a bit of water if necessary to keep the sauce loose, or remove the lid to evaporate and thicken it.

Meanwhile, in a medium saucepan, boil the green beans in lightly salted water until tender but still a bit crispy, 5 to 8 minutes. Drain.

Scatter the beans across the top of the chicken, add 2 to 3 Tbsp water if the sauce needs loosening, loosely cover, and cook for a final 10 minutes. Sprinkle some sesame seeds over the beans and serve.

This lush tagine is usually called by the general name *m'assal*, which means "caramelized"—sometimes done with sugar, sometimes with honey, sometimes with both—and is derived from the word *assal* (honey). Traditionally made with lamb, the dish is now a succulent way to prepare chicken. Serve with plenty of bread or a bowl of plain couscous (see page 171) on the side.

The tomato compote is made separately and spooned on the tagine before serving. It can be dusted with cinnamon and served on its own as a salad, ideally among a selection of diversely flavored salads. Depending on the natural sweetness of the tomatoes, some compotes might need a touch more honey.

CHICKEN TAGINE WITH CARAMELIZED TOMATO COMPOTE

djaj m'assal

SERVES 4

4 whole chicken legs

3 garlic cloves, minced

1 Tbsp finely chopped fresh flat-leaf parsley

1 Tbsp finely chopped fresh cilantro

1 tsp ground ginger

½ tsp turmeric

1 pinch saffron threads, dry-toasted and ground (see page 50)

Salt and freshly ground black pepper

¼ cup/60 ml olive oil

CARAMELIZED TOMATO COMPOTE

2 lb/910 g ripe medium tomatoes

1½ Tbsp olive oil

Salt

¼ cup/60 g sugar

2 Tbsp honey, plus more if needed

¼ tsp orange flower water or rose water

¼ tsp ground cinnamon

2 medium red onions, finely chopped

1 small cinnamon stick

24 unsalted toasted almonds without skins

Toasted sesame seeds for garnishing

CONTINUED

Rinse the chicken, remove the skin, and trim any excess fat. If desired, split the legs into drumsticks and thighs.

In a large mixing bowl, add the garlic, parsley, cilantro, ginger, turmeric, and saffron. Season with salt and pepper. Moisten with the olive oil and blend well. Add the chicken and turn to coat. Cover and marinate for 30 minutes, turning from time to time.

PREPARE THE CARAMELIZED TOMATO COMPOTE. Bring a pot of water to a boil. Fill a large bowl with cold or ice water. Cut out the stem ends from each tomato and cut an X in the bottoms. Place the tomatoes in the boiling water and cook until the skins begin to split, about 1 minute. Immediately transfer with a slotted spoon to the cold water. When the tomatoes are cool, peel them. Working over a bowl to catch all the juices, seed and core the tomatoes. Cut into quarters.

In a heavy skillet or sauté pan, heat the olive oil over medium heat. Add the tomatoes and their juices with a pinch of salt, and cook, stirring from time to time, until they turn darker, about 20 minutes. Add the sugar and cook for 5 minutes. Stir in the honey, orange flower water, and ground cinnamon and continue to cook until the tomatoes are deep red, pasty, and caramelized, 15 to 20 minutes. Taste for sweetness and, if needed, add more honey and cook for 5 minutes. Transfer to a bowl.

In a tagine, flameproof casserole, or large, heavy skillet or sauté pan, add the chicken and all the marinade. Spread the onions over the top. Cover and cook over medium heat until the chicken is browned, about 12 minutes, turning it from time to time. Add the cinnamon stick and 1 cup/240 ml water, loosely cover, and cook over medium-low heat, moving the chicken from time to time to keep it from sticking, until done but not falling off the bone, about 45 minutes. Stir in a bit of water if necessary to keep the sauce loose, or remove the lid to evaporate and thicken it.

In a small skillet, warm the almonds over medium-low heat until fragrant, about 2 minutes.

To serve, spoon the tomato compote over the chicken, scatter the almonds on top, and lightly sprinkle with sesame seeds.

Stewed in a sauce of butter (or, traditionally, the clarified, fermented butter known as *smen*), saffron, white pepper, almonds, and plenty of meltingly soft onions, this classic Fès chicken dish is rich, almost decadent. As opposed to many dishes where almonds are fried and scattered over the top for a crunchy touch, here blanched almonds are added raw and cooked in the sauce, resulting in a firm and slightly brittle texture.

CHICKEN IN BUTTERY SAFFRON-ONION SAUCE WITH ALMONDS

djaj khdra bil louz

SERVES 4

2 bone-in chicken breasts and 2 whole chicken legs (about 2½ lb/1.2 kg)
2 pinches saffron threads, dry-toasted and ground (see page 50)
¼ tsp freshly ground white pepper
4 medium red onions
3 Tbsp butter or *smen* (see page 45), softened
½ cup/60 g raw almonds, blanched and skins removed (see page 41)
Salt

Rinse the chicken, remove the skin, and trim any excess fat.

In a tagine, flameproof casserole, or large, heavy skillet or sauté pan, add the saffron, white pepper, and 2 Tbsp water and mix. Add the chicken and turn to coat. Finely chop one of the onions and add to the tagine. Add 2 Tbsp of the butter and the almonds and season with salt. Loosely cover and cook over medium heat until the chicken is browned, about 12 minutes, turning the pieces from time to time.

Halve the remaining onions and cut into ½-in-/ 12-mm-thick slices. Separate the sections and add to the tagine along with ½ cup/120 ml water. Loosely cover and cook over medium-low heat, moving the chicken from time to time to keep from sticking, until done but not falling off the bone, about 45 minutes. Stir in a bit of water if necessary to keep the sauce loose, or remove the lid to evaporate and thicken it.

Preheat the broiler.

Transfer the chicken to a platter to drain for a few minutes; return the juices to the tagine. Rub the chicken with the remaining 1 Tbsp of butter. Transfer to a baking sheet and broil until golden, 5 to 10 minutes.

Meanwhile, cook the sauce uncovered until reduced to a buttery-rich consistency, about 10 minutes.

Return the chicken to the tagine, cover with some sauce, and serve.

In this specialty of the Atlantic coast city of Essaouira, whisked eggs are poured over and around pieces of fragrant, braised chicken for the final 10 minutes or so of cooking. The result is a loose, yellowish green sauce thickened with set egg. I have adapted this *souiri* classic from one that talented Essaouira chef Khadija Benchaalal showed me on a summer afternoon at Villa Garnace in the city's medina, just inside the beefy, fortified ramparts. This boldly flavored chicken is excellent served with white rice and mint yogurt sauce (see page 140).

ESSAOUIRA-STYLE CHICKEN
BATHED IN
WHISKED EGGS

djaj souiri

SERVES 4

2 bone-in chicken breasts and 2 whole chicken legs (about 2½ lb/1.2 kg)

2 medium red onions, chopped

8 garlic cloves, minced

¼ cup/60 ml olive oil

½ preserved lemon (see page 45), quartered, seeded, rinsed, and chopped

2 Tbsp finely chopped fresh flat-leaf parsley

1 Tbsp ground ginger

2 tsp turmeric

Salt

4 large eggs

Rinse the chicken, remove the skin, and trim any excess fat. If desired, split the legs into drumsticks and thighs.

In a tagine, flameproof casserole, or large, heavy skillet or sauté pan, add the onions, garlic, olive oil, preserved lemon, 1 Tbsp of the parsley, the ginger, and turmeric. Season with salt. Cook over medium heat until fragrant, 4 to 5 minutes.

Add the chicken, turn to coat, and cook for 2 minutes on each side. Dribble 1 cup/240 ml water into the side of the tagine, stir, loosely cover, and cook over medium-low heat, moving the pieces from time to time, until the chicken is done but not falling off the bone, about 45 minutes. Remove the tagine from the heat, uncover, and let cool for 5 minutes.

In a bowl, whisk the eggs with a pinch of salt and the remaining 1 Tbsp parsley. Slowly pour the eggs over the chicken. Cover the tagine and cook over low heat until the eggs are set but still moist, about 10 minutes. Serve in the tagine.

FISH
AND
SHELLFISH

The country's long Atlantic and Mediterranean coastlines, plus a handful of rivers, offer Moroccan cooks an array of fish, from the popular sardines and conger eel to sea bass and various breams to Middle Atlas trout.

Often, before being cooked, fish is rubbed in a *charmoula* marinade prepared with fresh cilantro, garlic, paprika, cumin, salt, olive oil, and lemon juice. Regional preparations vary, with many northern cooks adding fresh parsley, thyme, and black pepper to their marinades.

Cooking fish in a tagine is popular along the coast. Traditionally, a layer of sliced carrots, celery leaves, or parsley stems lines the bottom of the tagine to keep the fish from sticking. Fish steaks or smaller fish like sardines are prepared in the tagine; larger whole fish are baked in the oven in a roasting pan. Moroccan cooks tend to refer to both methods as "tagine."

Among shellfish, shrimp—usually in a chile-and-garlic-laden tomato sauce (see page 156)—is popular, as is, in places, cuttlefish and calamari, the latter usually floured and deep-fried (see page 158). Mussels are especially prevalent in the southern coastal town of Sidi Ifni. In the markets, they are sold steamed and shucked, not in the shell. Inland from Sidi Ifni, in towns like Tiznit, Tan Tan, and Guelmim, spice merchants sell dried mussels, which need to be soaked overnight before being used in the same manner as fresh ones.

See page 55 for more information on cooking with tagines.

This excellent mussel dish comes from around Sidi Ifni—an isolated cliff-top town in the far south of Morocco that was under Spanish control for a century, until 1969—and is even simpler than the Mussel Tagine on page 154. It is also stronger in its Spanish influence. The classic *sofrito*—garlic, green pepper, and tomato base—is Spanish in texture and technique, but with the addition of cumin, the flavor is clearly Moroccan. People in Sidi Ifni eat this mussel dish with bread. It is also excellent over pasta or white rice.

Chef Malika Essaidi chops, rather than grates, the tomatoes in her version of the dish, as she prefers the added texture. That's just one of many subtle options possible.

MUSSELS IN TOMATO SAUCE

SERVES 4

5 lb/2.3 kg large mussels, rinsed and beards trimmed

2 Tbsp olive oil

1 sweet Italian green pepper or ½ green bell pepper, seeded, deribbed, and finely chopped

3 large garlic cloves, minced

6 ripe medium tomatoes, halved, seeded, and grated (see Note, page 78)

1 tsp sweet paprika

¾ tsp ground cumin

Salt and freshly ground black pepper

2 Tbsp finely chopped fresh flat-leaf parsley, plus more for garnishing

In a large pot, bring ½ cup/120 ml water to a boil over high heat. Add the mussels, cover, and steam until the mussels have opened, shaking the pot from time to time, 3 to 5 minutes. Tip into a colander to drain and cool. Discard any mussels that did not open. Shuck the mussels and then trim any remaining beards with scissors. There should be about 2 cups/480 ml shucked mussels.

In a medium skillet or sauté pan, heat the olive oil over medium heat. Add the green pepper and cook for 2 minutes until fragrant. Add the garlic and cook for 1 to 2 minutes until fragrant, being careful not to scorch the garlic. Add the tomatoes, paprika, and cumin. Season with salt and pepper and stir in ¼ cup/60 ml water. Cook at a perky simmer, stirring from time to time, until the tomatoes are a deeper red and pulpy, about 15 minutes.

Add the 2 Tbsp parsley and the mussels, reduce the heat to low, loosely cover, and cook for 10 minutes. Garnish with parsley and serve immediately.

An important weekly *souq* assembles on the old airstrip at the edge of Sidi Ifni's center, offering goods from around the Anti-Atlas region. There's also an active fish market in the town center each afternoon once the boats return to port. Among sardines and cuttlefish are tubs of mussels—not in their glistening black shells, but already steamed and shucked. They are prepared a couple of different ways—for instance, in a tagine as here or in tomato sauce (see page 153)—and are eaten as a main dish with bread.

This recipe comes from a small family hotel called La Suerte Loca ("Crazy Luck"), opened in 1939 by a Spaniard, bought in 1958 by a Moroccan man, and now run by his daughters. The chef among the sisters is Malika Essaidi, who taught me this dish one winter evening as a sandstorm blew up from the not-too-distant Sahara. The evening turned quickly from fresh and almost cool to muggy. The wooden shutters banged and the flags flapped briskly, muffling the sound of the surf below. A fine talc of dust coated the old floor tiles. We were on the seaside, but keenly aware of how close the desert loomed.

MUSSEL TAGINE

SERVES 4

5 lb/2.3 kg large mussels, rinsed and beards trimmed

4 Tbsp/60 ml olive oil

1 fat carrot, scrubbed and cut into ¼-in-/ 6-mm-thick rounds

1 small turnip, peeled and cut into long wedges

3 ripe medium tomatoes, 1 halved crosswise and sliced lengthwise, 2 halved, seeded, and grated (see Note, page 78)

¼ green bell pepper, seeded, deribbed, and sliced lengthwise

4 small garlic cloves, minced

2 Tbsp finely chopped fresh flat-leaf parsley

2 Tbsp finely chopped fresh cilantro

1½ tsp ground cumin

1 tsp sweet paprika

Salt and freshly ground black pepper

4 lemon slices

8 to 12 green olives, rinsed

In a large pot, bring ½ cup/120 ml water to a boil over high heat. Add the mussels, cover, and steam until the mussels have opened, shaking the pot from time to time, 3 to 5 minutes. Tip into a colander to drain and cool. Discard any mussels that did not open. Shuck the mussels and trim any remaining beards with scissors. There should be about 2 cups/480 ml shucked mussels.

In a medium tagine, heavy skillet, or sauté pan, add 3 Tbsp of the olive oil and swirl the pan to coat the bottom evenly. Cover the bottom with the carrot rounds and then arrange the turnip wedges like spokes. Place the mussels on top. Lay the sliced tomato and bell pepper on the mussels.

In a small mixing bowl, mix the grated tomato together with the garlic, parsley, cilantro, cumin, and paprika. Season with salt and pepper. Spoon over the vegetables and mussels. Rinse the bowl with ¼ cup/60 ml water and pour into the side of the tagine. Drizzle the remaining 1 Tbsp olive oil over the tomato sauce and top with the lemon slices and olives.

Loosely cover and cook over medium-low heat until the carrots and turnips are tender and the tomato sauce has darkened, about 1 hour. There should be a bit of watery sauce remaining. Remove the lid at the end if needed to reduce the sauce. Serve immediately.

Often called shrimp *al pip-pil*, this northern favorite can be either spicy in the sense of piquant, with plenty of cayenne pepper, or spicy in the sense of heavily seasoned, with garlic, cumin, sweet paprika, and a pinch of cayenne pepper, plus plenty of fresh cilantro and parsley. This recipe is the latter, though you can add firepower as desired. The shrimp can also be prepared in individual terra-cotta dishes and served as an appetizer.

Although I have eaten this tagine in numerous places along the coast, the finest was in Tétouan. It was in a small *riad* (guesthouse) called El Reducto, which had not long before been converted by a Spanish woman from a mansion that, in 1948, had been reformed for the Gran Vizier of Tétouan, Sidi Ahmed Abdelkrim Haddad. Wandering through Tétouan's dense, ancient, and inward-looking city, it is easy to forget how near it is to the Mediterranean.

SPICY
SHRIMP TAGINE

SERVES 4

2 Tbsp olive oil

4 ripe medium tomatoes, halved, seeded, and grated (see Note, page 78)

6 garlic cloves, minced

2 Tbsp finely chopped fresh flat-leaf parsley

2 Tbsp finely chopped fresh cilantro

1 tsp sweet paprika

¼ tsp cayenne pepper or more to taste

¼ tsp ground cumin

1 bay leaf

Salt and freshly ground black pepper

1½ lb/680 g large shrimp, peeled, tails left on (about ¾ lb/340 g peeled)

3 slices lemon, halved

In a tagine, flameproof casserole, or heavy skillet or sauté pan, add the olive oil, tomatoes, and garlic, and cook uncovered over medium heat until the tomatoes are a deeper red and pulpy, about 12 minutes.

Reduce the heat to low. Stir in the parsley, cilantro, paprika, cayenne, and cumin. Add the bay leaf and season with salt and pepper. Place the shrimp on top and cook for 1 minute, and then turn. Place the lemon slices around the edges of the tagine, dribble 2 Tbsp water in the side, cover with the lid, and cook for 10 minutes. Serve bubbling hot in the tagine.

Across much of Morocco, seafood is usually first marinated in herbs and spices before being floured and deep-fried. But in the north of the country, many cooks favor Spanish-style *fritura*, using only a light dusting of flour and salt. Sometimes a large quantity of fresh seafood—small sole and red mullet, whole shrimp, calamari—rather than one variety are fried this way. Such dishes are always served with lemon wedges, a wide saucer of tomato dipping sauce, and a big stack of bread. The dipping sauce is, in practice, more for the bread than the seafood, but is an integral part of any *fritura* meal.

DEEP-FRIED
CALAMARI
WITH TOMATO DIPPING SAUCE

SERVES 4

FOR THE TOMATO DIPPING SAUCE
4 ripe medium tomatoes
¼ garlic clove
2 Tbsp finely chopped fresh cilantro
2 pinches ground cumin
Salt and freshly ground black pepper

Flour for dredging
Salt
Oil for deep-frying
2¼ lb/1 kg small or medium calamari, cleaned
     and cut into ½-in-/12-mm-wide rings (about
     18 oz/500 g cleaned)
1 lemon, cut into wedges

PREPARE THE TOMATO DIPPING SAUCE. Bring a pot of water to a boil. Fill a large bowl with cold or ice water. Cut the stem ends from the tomatoes and cut an X in the bottoms. Place the tomatoes in the boiling water and cook until the skins begin to split, about 1 minute. Immediately transfer with a slotted spoon to the cold water. When the tomatoes are cool, peel them. Working over a bowl to catch the juices, seed and core the tomatoes.

In a blender or food processor, purée the tomatoes, garlic, cilantro, and cumin. Season with salt and pepper. Transfer to a bowl, cover, and refrigerate until chilled. Before serving, divide the dipping sauce among four shallow dishes.

Put flour in a bowl and season with salt. In a medium skillet or sauté pan over high heat, heat at least 1 in/2.5 cm of oil until the surface shimmers. Reduce the heat to medium-high.

Working in small batches, toss the calamari in the flour to coat, pat to shake off any excess flour, and fry until golden and tender, about 1 minute. Transfer with a slotted spoon to paper towels to drain. Season with salt and serve immediately with lemon wedges and the dipping sauce.

Along the lengthy Atlantic coastline, brochettes of marinated fish are a favorite way of enjoying the day's catch. Swordfish and monkfish are usually considered the best. I have also eaten brochettes made with generous pieces of a large *courbine* (or meagre, a large, elongated silver gray fish with a golden throat) in El Jadida and Tan Tan, blue shark in Safi, and monkfish or conger eel in Essaouira. All were excellent.

MARINATED
FISH BROCHETTES

SERVES 4 TO 6

½ medium red onion, grated

6 garlic cloves, minced

Heaped 2 Tbsp finely chopped fresh flat-leaf parsley

Heaped 2 Tbsp finely chopped fresh cilantro

½ tsp cayenne pepper

½ tsp sweet paprika

½ tsp ground cumin

Salt and freshly ground black pepper

2 Tbsp extra-virgin olive oil

Juice of 1 lemon

2 lb/910 g swordfish, monkfish, blue shark, or other firm, white-fleshed fish, boned and cut into ¾- to 1-in/2- to 2.5-cm cubes

2 green bell peppers, seeded, deribbed, and cut into 1-in/2.5-cm squares

1 lime, halved and cut into small triangular pieces

Oil for greasing pan

In a large mixing bowl, add the onion, garlic, parsley, cilantro, cayenne, paprika, and cumin. Season with salt and pepper. Moisten with the olive oil and lemon juice and blend well. Add the fish and turn to coat. Cover, refrigerate, and marinate for at least 30 minutes, turning occasionally.

Prepare skewers with four or five pieces of fish on each, interspersed with bell pepper. Cap each with a piece of lime.

If using a grill pan, skillet, or griddle, lightly oil and heat over high heat. If using a barbecue, prepare a fire and heat until the coals are glowing. If using a broiler, preheat the broiler.

Cook the brochettes, turning as needed with the help of a spatula in order to cook evenly on each side, until the fish is opaque throughout and firm to touch, about 5 minutes. Serve hot.

When Moroccan families head to the beach for the day in summer, many lug big pots of sardine balls to eat. This version of the festive family dish is adapted from a recipe by Rachid El Ouariti at the three-room Riad Le Mazagao, which stretches over the entrance to the medina in El Jadida.

Although fresh sardines are the most typical fish used—they are available and inexpensive, flavorful, and naturally oily, which results in moist fish balls—mackerel or whiting also work. Fresh tuna steaks make for a delicious and easy alternative, but can be a bit dry.

In Essaouira, I have eaten the fish balls served over a bed of cooked sliced carrots, which gave the dish an appealing sweet touch. In a saucepan, boil sliced carrots in lightly salted water until just tender, 8 to 10 minutes; drain. Place a layer of carrots on the platter or in the tagine, cover with tomato sauce, and then top with the fish balls.

FISH BALLS IN TOMATO SAUCE

serdine kwari

SERVES 4 TO 6

FOR THE FISH BALLS

3 lb/1.4 kg whole fresh sardines, mackerel, or whiting, or 1¼ lb/570 g tuna steaks (see Note)

2 garlic cloves, minced

Heaped 1 Tbsp finely chopped fresh flat-leaf parsley

Heaped 1 Tbsp finely chopped fresh cilantro

1 tsp ground cumin

1 tsp sweet paprika

½ tsp ground ginger

¼ cup/50 g uncooked white rice

Salt

FOR THE TOMATO SAUCE

1 Tbsp olive oil

2 garlic cloves, minced

4 ripe medium tomatoes, halved, seeded, and grated (see Note, page 78)

½ tsp ground cumin

½ tsp sweet paprika

¼ tsp ground ginger

2 bay leaves

Salt

1 sweet Italian green pepper or ½ green bell pepper, seeded, deribbed, and cut lengthwise into 1-in-/2.5-cm-wide strips

24 to 36 violet olives with pits

PREPARE THE FISH BALLS. If using sardines, scale, wash, and then fillet. Holding a sardine in one hand, rock the head back and then forward, and then pull outward, drawing out the innards. Open up the fish and pull out the spine. Remove any bones and, where possible, skin. Repeat with the remaining sardines. Rinse the fillets under cool running water and check again for bones. If using another fish variety, fillet and remove the skin. Rinse the fillets under cool running water and check for bones.

In a food processor, put the fillets, garlic, parsley, cilantro, cumin, paprika, and ginger and grind into a smooth, consistent paste. Transfer to a mixing bowl, blend in the rice, and season with salt.

PREPARE THE TOMATO SAUCE. In a large pot, flameproof casserole, or sauté pan, add the olive oil and garlic and cook over medium heat until fragrant, about 1 minute. Add the tomatoes, cumin, paprika, ginger, and bay leaves and season with salt. Cover and cook over medium-low heat until the tomatoes are a deeper red and pulpy, about 10 minutes. Stir in ½ cup/120 ml water.

Roll 1 Tbsp or so of the fish paste into a smooth ball about 1 in/2.5 cm in diameter. Place in the pot. Roll balls with the remaining paste, adding each to the pot. There should be about 32 total. Jiggle the pan to make room for the balls if necessary.

Swirl the pot to rotate the fish balls. Drizzle in 1 cup/240 ml water, lay the strips of green pepper on top, and bring to a low boil. Cover and cook over medium-low heat until the fish balls are done, about 40 minutes. Cut one open to check that the rice in the middle is cooked. Scatter the olives around the pot and cook uncovered until the sauce has thickened, about 10 minutes. Serve on a platter or in a tagine.

NOTE: *Reduce the spices slightly if using a fish milder than sardines. If using tuna, look for fattier pieces or add 2 Tbsp olive oil when grinding to help moisten.*

Locals called the native trout in the Middle Atlas around the Berber town of Azrou *hut al-wad*, "fish of the river." During the Protectorate era, the French began farming *truite* in local streams. Just outside Azrou is a top-notch farm called Truites de l'Atlas, where regional *auberges* and restaurants come to buy live trout. The French-era Hôtel Panorama, built in 1928 on the outskirts of town where it has a view over the valley, is one such loyal customer. Chef Mohamed Oumadan—cooking in these parts since 1959 and at the hotel for the past twenty years—showed me his favorite preparations for trout, including this one. It's flavorful but does not overpower the delicate taste of the fish.

A medium-size trout needs about 4 minutes per side to cook. If the fish is particularly thick, add another 1 minute or so per side. Only turn once. For a smoky flavor, place the stuffed fish in a grill basket and cook over embers.

GRILLED ATLAS TROUT STUFFED WITH GRATED CARROTS AND FRESH BAY LEAVES

SERVES 4

4 trout, cleaned, with heads and tails
   (about 2½ lb/1.2 kg total)
Salt and freshly ground black pepper
2 medium carrots, scrubbed and grated
12 small fresh bay leaves, bruised (see page 47)
Olive oil

Wash the fish and pat dry with paper towels. Rub salt and pepper inside the cavity.

In a small mixing bowl, put the carrots and season with salt and plenty of pepper. Fill each fish with 2 Tbsp of the mixture so that the cavity bulges slightly. Inside each fish, layer 3 bay leaves, overlapping them slightly.

Rub salt and pepper on the outside of each fish and then a small amount of olive oil.

Heat a large nonstick skillet over medium-high heat. Lay the fish in the pan and cook for 4 minutes. With a wide, thin spatula, gently turn the fish, and cook until done, another 4 minutes. Serve immediately.

Like many Moroccan cooks, Khadija Oualili in Asilah bakes her fish tagines in the oven when she buys whole fish, especially sea bass or a local type of white bream, in the market of this northwestern coastal town. She cuts two parallel gashes to the bone on each side, rubs them with marinade, and then arranges the fish in a large roasting pan on top of a layer of tomatoes and potatoes.

When she buys steaks cut from larger fish such as monkfish, hake, swordfish, conger eel, or blue shark, she cooks them in a terra-cotta tagine on the stove. She marinates the fish first and lines the tagine with a bed of sliced vegetables. Because the vegetables take longer to cook than the fish, they need to be partly cooked beforehand to keep the fish from overcooking and becoming mushy.

The tagine should be moist enough without adding water, but watch during cooking that it doesn't become dry.

FISH TAGINE
WITH VEGETABLES

SERVES 4

2 garlic cloves, minced

2 Tbsp finely chopped fresh flat-leaf parsley

2 Tbsp finely chopped fresh cilantro

1 tsp ground cumin

1 tsp sweet paprika

1 pinch cayenne pepper

1 pinch saffron threads, dry-toasted and
    ground (see page 50)

Salt and freshly ground black pepper

5 Tbsp/75 ml olive oil

1 Tbsp fresh lemon juice

2¼ lb/1 kg steak of bream, hake, swordfish,
    monkfish, or other firm, white-fleshed fish
    with few bones, each about 1 in/2.5 cm thick

2 fat carrots, scrubbed and cut into ¼-in-/
    6-mm-thick rounds

3 medium white rose potatoes, peeled and cut
    lengthwise into ¼-in-/6-mm-thick slices

1 sweet Italian green pepper or ½ green
    bell pepper, seeded, deribbed, and cut
    lengthwise into 1-in-/2.5-cm-wide strips

2 ripe medium tomatoes, cut crosswise into
    ¼-in-/6-mm-thick slices

8 to 12 olives with pits, rinsed

In a large mixing bowl, add the garlic, parsley, cilantro, cumin, paprika, cayenne, and saffron. Season with salt and pepper. Moisten with 3 Tbsp of the olive oil and the lemon juice and blend well. Add the fish and turn to coat. Cover, refrigerate, and marinate for at least 30 minutes, turning occasionally.

Meanwhile, in a saucepan, boil the carrots in lightly salted water until tender, about 10 minutes. Drain and reserve. In a large saucepan, boil the potatoes in lightly salted water until tender but not crumbling, about 10 minutes. Drain and reserve.

Heat a medium skillet over medium heat. Add the green pepper strips, sprinkle in 2 to 3 Tbsp water, cover, and steam until just soft, 3 to 5 minutes. Remove and reserve.

In a tagine, flameproof casserole, or large, heavy skillet or sauté pan, add the remaining 2 Tbsp olive oil and swirl the tagine to evenly coat the bottom. Cover the bottom with the carrot rounds. Top with most of the tomatoes and then with half of the potatoes. Lay the fish steaks on top and spoon any remaining marinade on the fish. Arrange the remaining potatoes tentlike around the sides of the tagine, interspersed with the green pepper strips. Lay the remaining tomatoes on top and then the olives.

Place over medium heat, loosely cover, and cook until the fish is opaque throughout, 30 to 45 minutes. Add 2 to 3 Tbsp water, if needed, to keep the fish moist. Serve in the tagine.

In Essaouira, Safi, and other port towns along the central Atlantic coast, the most popular fish tagine is prepared with conger eel and a dark, caramelized onion and raisin topping called *tfaya*. Conger, which is fatty and flavorful, and has few bones, is readily available and well liked, but monkfish is often considered the preferred (if more expensive) option. Allow plenty of time for the onions to slowly caramelize. For a quicker version, some cooks skip the onions and add only raisins to sweeten the dish.

SWEET MONKFISH TAGINE
WITH CARAMELIZED ONION AND RAISIN *TFAYA*

SERVES 4

2 garlic cloves, minced

2 Tbsp finely chopped fresh flat-leaf parsley

¼ tsp ground cinnamon

1 pinch ground ginger

1 pinch saffron threads, dry-toasted and
    ground (see page 50)

Salt and freshly ground black pepper

¼ cup/60 ml olive oil

1 tsp fresh lemon juice

2 lb/910 g bone-in monkfish or other
    firm white-fleshed fish, cut into
    1-in-/2.5-cm-thick steaks

FOR THE *TFAYA*

Scant ½ cup/60 g raisins

3 Tbsp olive oil

1½ lb/680 g medium red onions, sliced
    lengthwise

⅓ cup/75 ml honey

⅓ tsp ground ginger

½ small cinnamon stick

In a mixing bowl, add the garlic, parsley, cinnamon, ginger, and saffron. Season with salt and pepper. Moisten with the olive oil and lemon juice, and blend well. Dip the fish steaks in the marinade, turning until well coated. Cover, refrigerate, and marinate for 1 hour or until the *tfaya* is done.

MEANWHILE, PREPARE THE *TFAYA*. In a small mixing bowl, soak the raisins in warm water for 10 minutes; drain. In a large, heavy skillet or sauté pan, heat the olive oil over medium heat. Add the onions and cook, stirring frequently to separate the sections and keep them from scorching, until they soften, about 12 minutes. Stir in the honey, sprinkle in the raisins and ginger, and add the cinnamon stick. Cook uncovered over low heat, letting the onions gently bubble and stirring from time to time, until the onions are tender and caramelized, about 50 minutes. Remove from the heat.

In a tagine, flameproof casserole, or large, heavy skillet or sauté pan, lay in the fish steaks and spoon any remaining marinade over the top. Cook over medium heat, turning the steaks once, until nearly cooked through, about 8 minutes.

Cover the fish with the *tfaya* mixture, drizzle 2 to 3 Tbsp water around the edges if the pan is dry, loosely cover, and cook over low heat for 10 minutes. Serve immediately.

COUSCOUS

As elsewhere in North Africa, couscous is an identity dish in Morocco. It's served on Fridays for lunch when families gather for the week's most important meal, and it acts as an anchor for the family, even the community.

Couscous refers to both the "grains" of ground durum wheat and the dish itself. Traditionally, Moroccans use a two-tiered couscoussier to prepare the grains. The stew is placed in the bottom of the pot, and the grains go in the perforated, uncovered basket positioned snugly on top. The grains then cook in the flavorful steam rising from the stew. Outside the region, the most common way to make couscous is to prepare the stew in one pot and the "quick-cooking" grains in a separate dish. Done right, quick-cooking grains can be almost as light and fluffy as those prepared in the traditional manner.

Although there are some countrywide standards, including Seven Vegetable Couscous (page 180) and Couscous with Caramelized Onion and Raisin *Tfaya* (page 177), the stew depends on region, season, and family. Many couscouses are full of vegetables, but very rarely are they vegetarian. Meat—a piece of bone-in lamb or beef—or maybe chicken or, on occasion along the coast, fish (see page 184) gives the stew flavor.

To serve couscous, mound the grains on a platter and decoratively cover with the meat or fish and vegetables. Moroccans tend to serve the broth on the side, sometimes adding a ladle of the liquid to color the top layer of grains.

For more on the types and sizes of couscous, see page 42. For more on couscoussiers and their alternatives, see page 53.

Of the two ways to prepare couscous, one uses quick-cooking or instant couscous, the most common variety available outside North Africa. The other is the traditional method that steams the grains two or three times in a two-tiered couscoussier. In between steamings, the grains are rested and then the clumps are worked out with fingers in a wide, shallow dish called a *gsâa*. The recipe here steams the grains over water, but the timing is the same if done over a simmering stew.

Outside the region, about 2⅔ cups/510 g dried couscous grains is enough for four to six people. If desired, prepare more—a large mound of couscous is always impressive.

COUSCOUS GRAINS:
TWO METHODS OF PREPARING

QUICK-COOKING COUSCOUS

SERVES 4 TO 6

1 tsp sea salt
About 2⅔ cups/510 g couscous
1 Tbsp olive oil

In a measuring pitcher, add the salt to 2⅔ cups/ 630 ml warm water and stir until dissolved.

Pour the couscous into a very wide, shallow dish or *gsâa*. Sprinkle with the warm water and rake with the fingers or a fork. Let sit undisturbed for 15 minutes.

Check the grains. They should be tender but not mushy. If they are not yet tender, sprinkle with 2 to 3 Tbsp of the warm water and let sit for 5 to 10 minutes more, or until ready.

Drizzle the couscous with the olive oil. Using both hands, lift the grains and let them fall through your fingers. Work out any clumps by rubbing the grains gently between your palms.

Preheat the oven to 350°F/180°C/gas mark 4.

Transfer the couscous to a large baking dish and place in the oven. Heat the couscous, turning the grains occasionally, until they begin to steam, 10 to 15 minutes.

Pile the grains on a serving platter or *gsâa* and fluff with a fork. Fluff again before serving.

CONTINUED

STEAMING IN A COUSCOUSSIER

SERVES 4 TO 6

About 2⅔ cups/510 g couscous
1 tsp sea salt
1 Tbsp olive oil

In the bottom part of a couscoussier, bring 3 or 4 in/7.5 or 10 cm of water to a boil. Place a strip of aluminum foil or plastic wrap around the rim, and set the steaming basket snugly on top.

Meanwhile, pour the couscous into a very wide, shallow dish or *gsâa*. Sprinkle with ⅔ cup/165 ml cool water while raking with your fingers. Let the grains sit for 10 minutes. Using both hands, lift the grains and let them fall through your fingers. Work out any clumps by rubbing the grains gently between your palms.

A handful at a time, transfer the couscous to the top basket for the first steaming, rubbing the grains while doing so. Steam uncovered for 15 minutes; start the timing when the steam rises up through the couscous.

Dump the couscous into the dish, breaking up the grains and spreading them around with a wooden spoon. Sprinkle with the salt and 1⅓ cups/315 ml cool water. Work with your hands for 5 minutes, raking, rubbing, and sifting the grains to break up any lumps. Let rest for 5 minutes.

A handful at a time, transfer the couscous to the top basket for a second steaming, rubbing the grains while doing so. Steam uncovered for 15 minutes; start the timing when the steam rises up through the couscous.

Dump the couscous into the dish, breaking up the grains and spreading them around with the wooden spoon. Work with your hands for 5 minutes, raking, rubbing, and sifting the grains to break up any lumps.

Check the doneness of the grains. They should be tender but not mushy.

If the grains still have too much bite, sprinkle with ⅓ to ⅔ cup/75 to 165 ml cool water. Work the grains with your hands for 5 minutes, raking, rubbing, and sifting them to break up any lumps. Let rest for 5 minutes. A handful at a time, transfer the couscous to the top basket for a third steaming, rubbing the grains while doing so. Steam uncovered for 5 to 15 minutes; start the timing when the steam rises up through the couscous. Check for doneness from time to time. Dump the couscous into the dish, breaking up the grains and spreading them around with the wooden spoon.

Drizzle with the olive oil and work with the hands for 5 minutes, raking, rubbing, and sifting the grains to break up any lumps. Fluff before serving.

After crossing the 7,414-ft/2,260-m Tiz n'Tichka pass of the High Atlas, the road descends through a handful of small, earthen Berber villages and streamside terraces of barley. Planted in January and harvested in June, the fields of barley shimmer silvery green throughout the spring and summer. Barley was perhaps the original grain for couscous, used for centuries before the introduction of hard durum wheat. It's still widely used today in Berber areas. Barley couscous is darker and denser flavored, and a bit nutty.

This recipe comes from one of those high mountain villages, Tisseldeï, where Ahmed Agouni, a Berber who grew up in the village and went away to university to study geology, returned to open a most charming guesthouse called Irocha. Although this straightforward dish, full of vegetables and legumes, lacks the complex spices used in some parts of the Morocco, it is hearty and satisfying.

BERBER
BARLEY COUSCOUS
with VEGETABLES

SERVES 6

2 lb/910 g bone-in lamb leg, shoulder, or neck or beef shanks, cut into 6 or 8 pieces, or bone-in chicken with the skin pulled off and fat trimmed, cut into 6 or 8 pieces

1 lb/455 g medium onions, peeled and sliced lengthwise

4 ripe medium tomatoes, peeled, quartered, and seeded

1 Tbsp sweet paprika

1 tsp ground ginger

1 tsp ground cumin

1 pinch saffron threads, dry-toasted and ground (see page 50)

Salt and freshly ground black pepper

2 Tbsp olive oil

4 medium carrots, scrubbed, halved lengthwise and then crosswise

2 medium turnips, peeled and halved lengthwise

1 small bouquet fresh cilantro, tied

1 lb/455 g butternut squash, acorn squash, pumpkin, or another firm-fleshed, hard-skinned squash with peel, seeded, peel scrubbed, and cut into 3½-by-2-in/ 9-by-5-cm pieces

1 small eggplant, stemmed and quartered lengthwise

2 medium zucchini, halved lengthwise and then crosswise

Couscous Grains (page 171) prepared with barley couscous

CONTINUED

In the bottom of a couscoussier or large pot, put the meat, onions, tomatoes, paprika, ginger, cumin, and saffron. Season with salt and pepper. Add the olive oil and swirl to coat. Cover and cook over medium heat for 10 minutes.

Bring 5 cups/1.2 L water to a boil and pour into the pot. Loosely cover and cook for 45 minutes. Bring 4 cups/1 L water to a boil and add along with the carrots, turnips, and cilantro. Loosely cover and cook for 30 minutes. Add the squash, eggplant, and zucchini; loosely cover; and cook for a final 30 minutes. There should be about 4 or 5 cups /1 or 1.2 L of broth at the end. Discard the cilantro.

On a large serving platter or dish, gently mound the couscous and make a well in the center. Place the meat in the well and spread some of the vegetables around the couscous in an attractive pattern. Drizzle a ladleful of the broth evenly over top. Serve with the remaining broth in a bowl on the side as well as the remaining vegetables.

This classic couscous exemplifies the sophisticated and harmonious blending of the sweet with the savory. The broth and tender chicken—laden with a mixture of fragrant spices—are delectable, but the real star is the caramelized onion and raisin *tfaya* that tops the couscous grains like a regal, honeyed crown. The dish is delicious with cold glasses of *lben* (buttermilk).

COUSCOUS WITH CARAMELIZED ONION AND RAISIN *TFAYA*

kuskus tfaya

SERVES 6

FOR THE *TFAYA*

Scant ½ cup/60 g raisins

3 Tbsp olive oil

2 lb/910 g medium red onions, sliced lengthwise

½ cup/120 ml honey

½ tsp ground ginger

1 small cinnamon stick

2½ lb/1.2 kg bone-in chicken thighs, skin pulled off and fat trimmed

½ tsp ground ginger

1 generous pinch saffron threads, dry-toasted and ground (see page 50)

6 cloves

1 small cinnamon stick

Salt and freshly ground white pepper

1 Tbsp olive oil

10 sprigs fresh cilantro

10 sprigs fresh flat-leaf parsley

2 medium carrots, scrubbed and quartered lengthwise

2 medium turnips, peeled and halved lengthwise

½ cup/90 g canned chickpeas, rinsed

1 Tbsp butter

¾ cup/180 ml light olive oil or vegetable oil for frying

½ cup/60 g raw almonds, blanched and skins removed (see page 41)

Couscous Grains (page 171)

3 hard-boiled eggs, quartered lengthwise

CONTINUED

PREPARE THE *TFAYA*. In a small mixing bowl, soak the raisins in warm water for 10 minutes to soften; drain. In a large, heavy skillet or sauté pan, heat the olive oil over medium heat. Add the onions and cook, stirring frequently to separate the sections and keep them from scorching, until they soften, about 15 minutes. Stir in the honey, sprinkle in the raisins and ginger, and add the cinnamon stick. Cook uncovered over low heat, letting the onions gently bubble and stirring from time to time, until the onions are tender and caramelized, 55 to 70 minutes. Remove from the heat.

Meanwhile, in the bottom of a couscoussier or large pot, put the chicken, ginger, saffron, cloves, and cinnamon stick. Season with salt and white pepper. Add the olive oil and swirl to coat. Fold the cilantro and parsley in half, tie into a tight bundle with cotton kitchen string, and add along with the carrots, turnips, chickpeas, and butter. Cover with 4 cups/1 L water and bring to a boil over high heat. Reduce the heat to medium-low, loosely cover, and cook until the chicken is tender but not falling off the bone, about 45 minutes.

In a small saucepan, heat the oil for frying over medium-high heat. Add the almonds and fry, stirring to cook them evenly, until golden, 1 to 2 minutes. Transfer with a slotted spoon to paper towels to drain.

With a slotted spoon, transfer the chicken to a platter; cover and keep warm. Strain the broth into a bowl, picking out and reserving the chickpeas but discarding the vegetables, herbs, cinnamon stick, and cloves. Taste and adjust the seasoning as needed.

On a large serving platter or dish, gently mound the couscous and make a well in the center. Drizzle a ladleful of the broth evenly over top. Place the chicken in the well, cover with the *tfaya*, and top with the almonds. Arrange the hard-boiled eggs and some reserved chickpeas around the base of the couscous. Serve with the remaining broth in a bowl on the side.

Some call this Morocco's national dish. The best, many claim, comes from Casablanca—the country's largest city and financial capital—and Rabat—its political capital. There should be seven different kinds of vegetables, which can vary depending on the season. The many vegetables contribute excellent flavor, but the figure is not random: seven is an auspicious number throughout Islam.

If using dried chickpeas instead of canned chickpeas, soak overnight, drain, and place in the pot when adding water the first time.

SEVEN VEGETABLE COUSCOUS

kuskus baydawi

SERVES 6

1 lb/455 g bone-in lamb leg, shoulder, or neck or beef shanks, cut into 6 or 8 pieces, or bone-in chicken with the skin pulled off and fat trimmed, cut into 6 or 8 pieces

2 medium onions, quartered

4 ripe medium tomatoes, quartered and seeded

1 Tbsp sweet paprika

1 pinch saffron threads, dry-toasted and ground (see page 50)

Salt and freshly ground black pepper

2 Tbsp olive oil

1 Tbsp butter

4 medium carrots, scrubbed and halved lengthwise and then crosswise

2 medium turnips, peeled and halved lengthwise

1 tsp tomato paste

12 sprigs fresh flat-leaf parsley

12 sprigs fresh cilantro

½ head medium cabbage (about 1½ lb/ 680 g), quartered into wedges

1 lb/455 g butternut squash, acorn squash, pumpkin, or another firm-fleshed, hard-skinned squash with peel, seeded, peel scrubbed, and cut into roughly 3-by-2-in/ 7.5-by-5-cm pieces

2 medium zucchini, halved lengthwise and then crosswise

About 1 cup/170 g canned chickpeas, rinsed

Scant ½ cup/60 g raisins

Couscous Grains (page 171)

In the bottom of a couscoussier or large pot, put the meat, onions, tomatoes, paprika, and saffron. Season with salt and pepper. Add the olive oil, swirl to coat, and then add the butter. Cover and cook over medium heat for 10 minutes.

Bring 5 cups/1.2 L water to a boil and pour into the pot. Loosely cover and cook for 40 minutes. Bring 4 cups/1 L water to a boil and add along with the carrots, turnips, and tomato paste. Fold the parsley and cilantro sprigs in half, tie into a tight bundle with cotton kitchen string, and add to the pot. Loosely cover and cook for 30 minutes. Add the cabbage, loosely cover, and cook for 20 minutes. Add the squash, zucchini, chickpeas, and raisins; loosely cover; and cook for a final 30 minutes. There should be 4 to 5 cups/ 1 to 1.2 L broth at the end. Discard the parsley and cilantro.

With a slotted spoon, gently transfer the vegetables to a large platter. On a large serving platter or dish, gently mound the couscous and make a well in the center. Place the meat in the well, spread the vegetables around the couscous in an attractive pattern, and scatter the chick-peas and raisins around the base. Drizzle a ladle-ful of the broth evenly over the top. Serve with the remaining broth and vegetables in bowls on the side.

Most of the country's pumpkins and hard squashes come from around El Jadida. In the rural south, farmers with small plots of land sell stacks of these vegetables in various shades of greens and oranges from roadside stalls.

This delicious couscous combines the rustic taste of squash with a touch of sweetness from the raisins and ginger. The raisins can be boiled in the pot, but when they are cooked separately in butter with the almonds and sprinkled across the top of the finished dish, the pairing adds a lovely final texture. Use large pieces of squash with the thick skin intact so that they keep their shape. If desired, to make the squash easier to eat, cut off the skin and reduce the cooking time for the squash by 5 minutes. Adding a handful of canned chickpeas with the pieces of squash is a delicious accompaniment.

COUSCOUS
WITH PUMPKIN

SERVES 6

2 lb/910 g bone-in lamb leg, shoulder, or neck or beef shanks, cut into 6 or 8 pieces, or bone-in chicken with the skin pulled off and fat trimmed, cut into 6 or 8 pieces

3 medium onions, halved

1 tsp ground ginger

2 pinches saffron threads, dry-toasted and ground (see page 50)

10 black peppercorns

Salt

2 Tbsp olive oil

15 sprigs fresh flat-leaf parsley

15 sprigs fresh cilantro

2 medium carrots, scrubbed

2 medium turnips, scrubbed and halved lengthwise

2 lb/910 g pumpkin squash or butternut squash, seeded, peel scrubbed, and cut into 6 or 8 large pieces

Scant ¼ cup/30 g raisins

1 Tbsp butter

½ cup/60 g unsalted toasted almonds without skins

Couscous Grains (page 171)

In the bottom of a couscoussier or large pot, put the meat, onions, ginger, saffron, and peppercorns. Season with salt. Add the olive oil and swirl to coat. Cover and cook over medium heat for 10 minutes.

Fold the parsley and cilantro sprigs in half, tie into a tight bundle with cotton kitchen string, and add to the pot along with the carrots and turnips. Cover with 4 cups/1 L water and bring to a boil over high heat. Reduce the heat, loosely cover, and cook for 1 hour.

Bring 3 cups/720 ml water to a boil and add to the pot with the pumpkin. Loosely cover and cook for a final 30 minutes.

Soak the raisins in warm water for 10 minutes to soften; drain.

In a small saucepan, melt the butter over medium-low heat. Add the almonds and raisins and cook, stirring frequently, until the almonds are golden and the raisins puffed up, about 3 minutes. Remove from the heat.

Carefully strain the broth into a bowl; there should be 4 to 5 cups/1 to 1.2 L. Pick out and reserve the pumpkin but discard the onions, carrots, turnips, parsley, and cilantro.

On a large serving platter or dish, gently mound the couscous and make a well in the center. Place the meat in the well and gently cover the sides with pieces of pumpkin. Drizzle a ladleful of the broth evenly over the top. Scatter the almonds and raisins over the top. Serve with the remaining broth in a bowl on the side.

A wide range of fish can be used for this couscous, but it's important that the fish has few bones, or at least large ones that are easy to remove. That means fillets or steaks. Use fillets that have the skin still on, which helps keep them from flaking apart. Fillets from medium sea bream are perfect.

This recipe is loosely adapted from one made by Zoubida Azouzi. She lives in Tiznit, a key transit city between the deep south and the Sahara and the rest of the country, not far inland from the sea. Zoubida cooks at the Bab el Maâder guesthouse within the city's sturdy, 4-mi/6.5-km circuit of pounded earth-and-straw *pisé* walls. She prepares the fish, preferably *courbine*, or meagre, in one pot and the broth in a couscoussier, over which she steams the couscous grains. Unless you are steaming the couscous over the broth, you can use a single pot and gently slip the fillets or steaks into the broth at the end to poach the fish.

FISH COUSCOUS

kuskus hut

SERVES 6

2 Tbsp finely chopped fresh flat-leaf parsley
2 small garlic cloves, minced
2 tsp sweet paprika
1 tsp ground cumin
Salt and freshly ground black pepper
4 Tbsp/60 ml olive oil
1½ to 2 lb/680 to 910 g large skin-on bream, sea bass, cod, or grouper fillets, cut into 6 portions, or 3 lb/1.4 kg bream, hake, swordfish, or monkfish steaks
1 medium onion, finely chopped

3 ripe medium tomatoes, halved, seeded, and grated (see Note, page 78)
½ Tbsp turmeric
1 pinch cayenne pepper
4 medium carrots, scrubbed and halved lengthwise and then crosswise
2 small turnips, peeled and halved lengthwise
2 medium zucchini, scrubbed and halved lengthwise and then crosswise
Couscous Grains (page 171)

In a mixing bowl, add the parsley, garlic, 1 tsp of the paprika, and the cumin. Season with salt and pepper. Moisten with 2 Tbsp of the olive oil and blend well. Place the fish in the marinade and turn to coat. Cover and refrigerate, turning occasionally, until ready to cook.

In the bottom of a couscoussier or large pot, put the remaining 2 Tbsp olive oil, the onion, and tomatoes and cook over medium heat until the tomatoes are a deeper red and pulpy, about 10 minutes. Stir in the remaining 1 tsp paprika, the turmeric, and cayenne. Season with salt and add the carrots and turnips. Cover with 5 cups/1.2 L water and bring to a boil over high heat. Reduce the heat to medium-low, loosely cover, and cook at a low boil for 1 hour. Lay the zucchini in the broth and cook for 15 minutes.

Remove the fish from the marinade, discarding any excess marinade. Gently lay the fillets in the broth and cook until opaque throughout, 5 to 15 minutes depending on the fish. Baste occasionally with the liquid using a ladle or by gently swirling the pot.

With a slotted spoon, very carefully transfer the fish to a platter and then the vegetables. Strain the broth and taste for seasoning, adjusting as needed. On a large serving platter or dish, gently mound the couscous and make a well in the center. Place the fish in the well, and spread the vegetables around the couscous in an attractive pattern. Drizzle a ladleful of the broth evenly over the top. Serve with the remaining broth in a bowl on the side.

SWEETS AND DESSERTS

Stewed Sweet Spiced Pears
• 189 •

Oranges with
Orange Flower Water
and Cinnamon
• 190 •

Orange Slices with
Anise, Ginger,
and Golden Raisins
• 192 •

Stuffed Dates
• 193 •

Honeyed Phyllo Triangles
Stuffed with Almonds
briouats biz louz
• 195 •

Crispy Pastry with
Orange Flower Custard
and Almonds
pastilla jouhara
• 196 •

Milk Pudding
with Sliced Almonds
m'halbi
• 198 •

Ground Almond, Honey,
and Argan Oil Dip
amlou
• 199 •

Ghriba Walnut Cookies
• 200 •

Double-Baked Anise and
Sesame Seed Cookies
fekkas beldi
• 202 •

Clementine Sponge Cake
with Clementine Glaze
• 203 •

Sweet Couscous
seffa
• 205 •

Sweets are fundamental to Moroccan culture and form an important part of the culinary experience. They are served not only at the end of a meal but also before a meal with mint tea. Trays of delicacies are offered to welcome guests at ceremonies and fetes—births, engagements, weddings—and religious celebrations. Neighbors and family members send sweets to each other and simply enjoy them regularly with tea, coffee, or juice. Every day and every invitation includes sweets.

A symbol of the refined nature of Moroccan cuisine, sweets offer a tasty glimpse of the country's rich gastronomic heritage. A dip of ground almonds, honey, and argan oil (see page 199) originated in the Berber Anti-Atlas. Delicate sweetmeats reveal influences from Arabs from the Middle East and Jewish and Muslim refugees from Spain in the fifteenth and sixteenth centuries. Middle Eastern-inflected milk pudding (see page 198) is yet another piece in the cultural and culinary mosaic.

Some favorites are fruit based, including seasoned orange slices (see page 190 and page 192), stewed spiced pears (see facing page), and dates stuffed with almond paste (see page 193).

I have tasted this countrywide favorite of stewed pears in numerous places from north to south, but no more memorably than the version Bahija Lafridi prepared at the elegant Jnane Tamsna in Marrakech's *palmeraie* (palm grove). The pears were firm and sweet, glowed a lovely golden hue, and hinted of citrus and the exotic spices of trans-Saharan caravan routes that once passed through Marrakech. The grounds of the large estate, densely planted with everything from medicinal botanicals to fruit trees, owe much to ancient, sophisticated Arab-Andalusian horticulture traditions. This recipe is adapted from a fine memory of that early summer day dining in the shade of palms and pistachio trees.

STEWED SWEET
SPICED PEARS

SERVES 6

6 ripe but quite firm pears such as Anjou, Bosc, Conference, or Bartlett (about 3 lb/1.4 kg)
Generous 1 cup/225 g sugar
1½ cups/360 ml fresh orange juice
1 small cinnamon stick, broken into pieces, or 4 or 5 small pieces cinnamon bark
¼ tsp ground ginger
10 cardamom pods, gently crushed
6 cloves
6 sprigs fresh mint for garnishing

Peel the pears without removing the stems, leaving the fruits whole. Trim the bottom of each pear so that it can stand upright.

In a large sauté pan, add the sugar to ⅓ cup/75 ml water. Cook over medium heat until the sugar has caramelized and is a deep amber color, 6 to 8 minutes. Remove from the heat. Carefully pour in the orange juice and add the cinnamon,

ginger, cardamom, and cloves, stirring to dissolve the caramelized sugar that hardened when the juice was added.

Place the pears upright in the pan. Bring to a low boil over medium heat, reduce the heat to low, and simmer uncovered until the pears are golden yellow and tender but not mushy, 30 to 35 minutes. As the pears cook, gently roll them onto their sides and swirl the pan from time to time so that they cook—and take on color—evenly in the liquid.

Carefully remove the pears by picking them up by the stems and cupping the bottoms with a spoon. Set upright on small dessert plates. Drizzle a small amount of the sauce over the pears along with the spices, letting the sauce pool around the base of the pears. Serve at room temperature or a little warm. Garnish with the mint sprigs.

One of the most popular desserts around the country is made with fresh oranges. Cut into slices and sweetened with sugar and orange flower water, they are chilled and then dusted with cinnamon before serving. This simple dessert is utterly delicious, especially with a plate of *Ghriba* Walnut Cookies (page 200) or Double-Baked Anise and Sesame Seed Cookies (page 202).

ORANGES WITH ORANGE FLOWER WATER AND CINNAMON

SERVES 4

4 plump Valencia oranges
1 tsp superfine sugar
⅛ tsp orange flower water
Ground cinnamon for dusting
4 sprigs fresh mint for garnishing

Trim off the top and bottom ends of the oranges and reserve. Peel each orange with a knife, removing any of the white pith around the fruits. Cut crosswise into ⅓-in-/8-mm-thick slices. Transfer to a mixing bowl.

In a small mixing bowl, squeeze the juice from the reserved ends. Add the sugar, orange flower water, and a pinch of cinnamon and whisk until the sugar is dissolved. Pour over the orange slices, turning to coat. Cover and refrigerate until chilled.

Divide the oranges among four dessert plates, overlapping the slices. Spoon any remaining juice over the top and dust with cinnamon. Garnish with the mint sprigs and serve.

This slightly bolder version of the classic dessert Oranges with Orange Flower Water and Cinnamon (page 190) substitutes ginger and aniseeds for the cinnamon. I first tasted it at Dar Nour in Tanger. Soak the raisins only long enough to soften them. They should not be allowed to get pasty and pruney. Prepare the dessert before the meal to give the oranges time to chill and the flavors to meld.

ORANGE SLICES WITH ANISE, GINGER, AND GOLDEN RAISINS

SERVES 4

Scant ¼ cup/30 g golden raisins
4 plump Valencia oranges
Superfine sugar for sprinkling
¼ tsp aniseeds
Ground ginger for dusting
4 sprigs fresh mint for garnishing

In a small mixing bowl, soak the raisins in tepid water for 5 minutes to soften; drain.

Trim off the top and bottom ends of the oranges and reserve. Peel the oranges with your fingers, removing as much of the white pith around the fruits as possible. Cut each orange crosswise into five or six slices about ½ in/12 mm thick. Divide among four dessert plates, overlapping the orange slices as little as possible.

Squeeze the juice from the reserved ends over the slices. On each slice, sprinkle one pinch of sugar and five or six aniseeds. Dust each plate with two pinches of ginger and scatter a scant 1 Tbsp raisins over each serving. Cover and refrigerate until well chilled. Garnish with the mint sprigs and serve.

Dates are revered, and much enjoyed, in Morocco. Of the more than two hundred varieties that the country produces, large *mejhoul* dates are the ones used for special occasions and special recipes like these stuffed dates. Typically, the almond paste is much sweeter than in this recipe, and the stuffed date is rolled in sugar. I prefer to let the dates' natural and intense sweetness shine.

To make the dates festive, many Moroccan cooks work some food coloring—red, green, yellow, even blue—into the almond paste before stuffing it inside the dates.

STUFFED DATES

MAKES 12 STUFFED DATES

¾ cup/100 g ground almonds

3 Tbsp powdered sugar

2 tsp orange flower water

Food coloring (optional)

12 *mejhoul* dates or other large, sweet date variety with pits

12 walnut halves or 12 unsalted toasted almonds without skins

In a mixing bowl, add the ground almonds, powdered sugar, and orange flower water. Add 1 Tbsp water and work into a paste. The dough should be slightly moist; add a few more drops of water (or orange flower water) if needed.

If using food coloring, divide the paste into even parts, add 5 or 6 drops of a single color to each, and work in.

Wipe the dates with a damp cloth. Cut a lengthwise incision across the top of each date and carefully remove the pit. Take 1 tsp or so of the almond paste, roll it between your palms into a spherical shape, and tuck inside the date. It should bulge out of the opening. Repeat with the remaining paste and dates. Garnish each date with a walnut pressed slightly edgewise into the almond paste before serving.

These almond-stuffed pastries soaked in honey can be called the queen of Moroccan sweets. Whether bite-size or large ones that take a few bites to eat, whether sprinkled with sesame seeds or crushed almonds, they're invariably sticky, filling, and delicious.

HONEYED PHYLLO TRIANGLES STUFFED WITH ALMONDS

briouats bil louz

MAKES ABOUT 16 TRIANGLES

1¼ cups/170 g unsalted toasted almonds without skins, crushed, plus more for garnishing

About ⅔ cup/80 g powdered sugar

1 large egg, separated

1 tsp orange flower water

2 pinches ground cinnamon

4 sheets phyllo dough or *warqa* (see page 46), plus more in case of breakage

Olive oil for brushing

1 cup/240 ml honey

Light olive oil or vegetable oil for frying

In a mixing bowl, blend the crushed almonds with the powdered sugar, egg white, orange flower water, and cinnamon. In a small bowl, whisk the egg yolk.

On a clean, flat work surface, unroll the phyllo sheets. Cut into strips about 3 in/7.5 cm wide and at least 9 in/23 cm long. Arrange a couple of the strips facing away from you; cover the remaining strips with plastic wrap to keep them from drying out. Lightly brush the strips with olive oil.

Place a heaped 1 Tbsp of the almond filling on the end of each strip closest to you. Fold over to form a triangle, then fold again to form another triangle, and so on to the end. Brush the end of the triangle with egg yolk and fold the loose end over the brushed yolk. Place the triangles on a plate without letting them touch. Repeat with the remaining almond filling and phyllo sheets.

In a saucepan, warm the honey over low heat until runny; keep warm. Place a strainer over a bowl.

In a large skillet or sauté pan over high heat, heat at least ½ in/12 mm of oil until the surface shimmers; reduce the heat to medium. Working in small batches, gently place the phyllo triangles in the hot oil and fry, turning once, until golden brown, 30 seconds to 1 minute. Transfer with a slotted spoon to paper towels to drain for a few minutes. Carefully transfer the pastries to the honey and let sit for about 5 minutes, turning them once or twice. Transfer the pastries to the strainer to drain for about 5 minutes. (Reuse the drained honey if needed.)

Lay the pastries on a wide platter without letting them touch. Sprinkle with more crushed almonds and serve at room temperature.

Rounds of crisp, delicate pastry layered with custard make a delicious and festive dish that is traditional for celebrations. This recipe for individual desserts is loosely adapted from a version made at Riad el Amine, a centuries-old mansion in Fès that once belonged to the grandparents of the owner, Jawhar Yassir. When I asked him how his grandmother used to make the custard, he immediately telephoned her. "Exactly the same," she told him, "but without the cornstarch." She thought that was cheating a little, making the custard easier to thicken.

Phyllo is brittle, and once it is cut into rounds, the pastry tends to curl at the edges. The rounds are easier to stack when flat, so after cutting the pastry, leave the rounds covered with a kitchen cloth until brushing them with oil and baking them. Prepare a few more sheets than needed in case the phyllo breaks or curls excessively.

The phyllo and the custard can be prepared in advance and the dessert assembled just before serving.

CRISPY PASTRY WITH ORANGE FLOWER CUSTARD AND ALMONDS

pastilla jouhara

SERVES 4

½ lb/225 g phyllo dough sheets or *warqa* (see page 46)
Olive oil for brushing
About ½ cup/60 g sliced almonds
1½ cups/360 ml cold milk
1½ Tbsp cornstarch

2 tsp orange flower water
2 large eggs
3 Tbsp sugar
Seasonal fresh fruit, such as raspberries or sliced strawberries, for garnishing
4 sprigs fresh mint for garnishing

Preheat the oven to 350°F/180°C/gas mark 4.

Brush the phyllo sheets lightly with olive oil and stack in layers of three sheets. Using a 3-in-/7.5-cm-diameter cutter or an inverted glass and knife, cut out circles. Cover the cut circles with a kitchen cloth until ready to use.

Brush both sides of the phyllo rounds with olive oil. Arrange in a single layer on two or three baking sheets. Bake until golden and crispy, about 5 minutes. Carefully transfer the rounds to a rack to cool.

Spread the almonds in a cake pan and bake, shaking the pan from time to time, until golden, 2 to 4 minutes. Watch carefully that they do not burn.

In a saucepan, whisk the milk with the cornstarch and orange flower water. In a mixing bowl, beat the eggs and sugar until spongy and then whisk into the milk. Cook over medium-low heat, stirring continually with a wooden spoon, until the mixture thickens and coats the back of the spoon, about 8 minutes. Do not let the custard reach a boil. Pass through a fine-mesh sieve or chinois into a bowl; discard any solids. Let cool. The custard should be thick enough to spoon onto the pastry rounds without running off.

Just before serving, on top of each dessert plate, dollop 1 Tbsp custard. Top with a pastry round, dollop with another 1 Tbsp custard, and then sprinkle with some almonds. Cover with another round, and top with 1 Tbsp custard and some nuts. Continue until there are four layers, ending with the custard and almonds. Surround the stacks with fruit and garnish with mint sprigs. Serve immediately.

This creamy dessert is not cloyingly sweet but tastes almost fresh. It is often associated with the Middle East, but one Moroccan told me that it has been made "ours" by often adding ingredients such as rose water or almonds instead of pistachios. In Rabat, I had a version of the pudding with a half-dozen threads of local saffron stirred into the bowl. The saffron gave the pale-colored pudding not only a distinctive flavor but also vibrant patches of yellow where the color bled from the threads.

The garnish of toasted sliced almonds offers a nice balance in taste and texture, but feel free to make the pudding "yours" by spreading, say, a spoonful of a favorite preserve or marmalade on top before scattering the almonds.

MILK PUDDING
WITH
SLICED ALMONDS

m'halbi

SERVES 4

2½ cups/600 ml milk
3 Tbsp sugar
⅓ cup/45 g cornstarch
About ¼ cup/30 g sliced almonds
Ground cinnamon for dusting

In a heavy saucepan, bring the milk and sugar to a simmer over medium heat. In a small mixing bowl, whisk the cornstarch with 3 Tbsp water to make a runny paste. Slowly add to the milk while stirring with a wooden spoon. Cook, stirring continually, until the mixture thickens, 1 to 2 minutes. Remove from the heat.

Pass the pudding through a fine-mesh sieve or chinois into a bowl. Divide among four dessert bowls, flan cups, or short, fat glasses. Let cool. Cover and refrigerate until chilled and set.

Preheat the broiler. Spread the almonds in a cake pan. Broil, shaking the pan from time to time, until golden, 1 to 2 minutes. Watch carefully that the nuts don't burn.

Just before serving, scatter the almonds over the puddings and dust with cinnamon.

In the southern Souss region in the Anti-Atlas, three local products are ground together to make a simple and exquisite dip for bread. The process of producing oil from indigenous argan tree nuts is labor-intensive and nowadays done almost exclusively at rural women's co-ops (see page 41 for more on argan oil). The best substitution is walnut oil, though extra-virgin olive oil also works. This dip for fresh bread is enjoyed at breakfast or for a midmorning or afternoon snack with Mint Tea (page 210) or Saffron Tea (page 211).

GROUND
ALMOND, HONEY,
AND ARGAN OIL DIP

amlou

MAKES ABOUT I CUP/240 ML

¾ cup/115 g unsalted toasted almonds without skins

6 Tbsp/90 ml argan oil, walnut oil, or extra-virgin olive oil, plus more if needed

¼ cup/60 ml honey, plus more if needed

In a food processor, add the almonds, oil, and honey and, using quick pulses, process until thoroughly blended. Alternatively, using quick pulses, grind the almonds, making sure that they do not turn pasty, then transfer to a small mixing bowl and work in the oil and then the honey with a fork until thoroughly blended. The texture should be gritty and the consistency loose and oily. Taste and add more oil or honey if needed.

Spoon into a bowl and serve.

Among Moroccan sweets, *ghriba* cookies stand out for their distinctive cracked surfaces. There are *ghribas* with almonds, with sesame seeds, with aniseeds, and these, a favorite, made largely with walnuts. With their rich, nutty taste and chewy texture, they are an ideal accompaniment to a plate of Oranges with Orange Flower Water and Cinnamon (page 190) or Orange Slices with Anise, Ginger, and Golden Raisins (page 192) and cups of Spiced Coffee (page 209).

GHRIBA
WALNUT COOKIES

MAKES ABOUT 2 DOZEN COOKIES

1 large egg
½ Tbsp butter, softened
¼ cup/50 g granulated sugar
1 pinch ground cinnamon
3 Tbsp all-purpose flour
1 tsp baking powder
2¼ cups/225 g walnut pieces, coarsely ground
Powdered sugar for dredging and dusting

In a large mixing bowl, beat the egg and butter, and then blend in the granulated sugar and cinnamon. In a small mixing bowl, mix together the flour and baking powder and work into the batter along with the walnuts. Mix to form a consistent, smooth dough. Cover and refrigerate until chilled.

Preheat the oven to 350°F/180°C/gas mark 4.

Place the powdered sugar in a bowl. Line a baking sheet with parchment paper.

Roll the dough into 1-in/2.5-cm balls. Roll the balls in the powdered sugar and place on the baking sheet, spacing them about 1 in/2.5 cm apart. Bake for 4 minutes, rotate the sheet, and bake until the cookies are golden and firm at the edges and cracked on the surface but soft in the center, another 3 to 5 minutes.

Remove from the oven and let cool on the sheet, then transfer to a rack. If desired, dust with more powdered sugar before serving.

These crunchy biscotti-like cookies are perfect served with Mint Tea (page 210) or Spiced Coffee (page 209). Pâtisseries prepare them with almonds, dates, raisins, or dried figs, but this recipe is the classic Moroccan version. The alluring orange flower water aroma and sesame seed and anise flavors make clear why many add the suffix *beldi*, meaning "local" or "of the country."

After the first baking, the logs need to be cooled completely before they are sliced and baked a second time. Allow perhaps a couple of hours for this.

DOUBLE-BAKED
ANISE and SESAME SEED COOKIES

fekkas beldi

MAKES ABOUT 40 COOKIES

2 large eggs, plus 1 egg white, lightly beaten

6 Tbsp/90 g sugar

2 Tbsp butter, melted

1 Tbsp orange flower water

1¾ cups/250 g all-purpose flour

2 tsp baking powder

About ⅓ cup/40 g toasted sesame seeds

1 Tbsp aniseed

1 pinch salt

Oil for moistening hands

Preheat the oven to 350°F/180°C/gas mark 4. Line a baking sheet with parchment paper.

In a mixing bowl, whisk the whole eggs and sugar, and then work in the butter and orange flower water. In another mixing bowl, blend the flour, baking powder, sesame seeds, aniseed, and salt. Add the flour mixture to the egg mixture, mixing to form a smooth, slightly sticky dough.

Working with oiled hands to keep the dough from sticking, divide the dough in half. Roll into two logs about 1½ in/4 cm in diameter. Place the logs on the baking sheet. Using a pastry brush, lightly paint with the egg white.

Bake the logs until golden and firm but still a bit soft to the touch, 20 to 25 minutes. Transfer the logs and the parchment paper to a rack to cool completely.

Again preheat the oven to 350°F/180°C/gas mark 4.

With a bread knife, cut the logs diagonally into ½-in-/12-mm-thick slices. Reline the baking sheet as well as a second sheet with parchment paper. Spread the cookies flat on the sheets. Bake until golden and crunchy, turning once if needed, about 15 minutes. Cool on racks. Store in an airtight container at room temperature for up to 1 week.

Although this cake shows the strong influence from the time when the country was a Protectorate under French and Spanish rule, it's clearly Moroccan. My favorite version came topped with a syrupy glaze made with clementine juice and had pieces of candied clementine slices inside. The cake was even more enjoyable with a large bowl of café au lait for breakfast.

The glaze is sweet, and each piece of cake only needs a dollop. Serve the remaining glaze on the side. Clementines are a delicious, sweet variety of mandarin orange. For the glaze, substitute mandarin juice or the juice of another variety, such as tangerines or even oranges.

CLEMENTINE SPONGE CAKE
WITH CLEMENTINE GLAZE

SERVES 10

1 cup/210 g butter, softened
1 cup/200 g sugar
4 large eggs
¼ cup/60 ml fresh clementine juice
1½ cups/200 g all-purpose flour
3 tsp baking powder

FOR THE CLEMENTINE GLAZE
1 cup/240 ml fresh clementine juice
1 cup/200 g sugar
1 clementine, scrubbed

Preheat the oven to 350°F/180°C/gas mark 4. Butter a 10-in/25-cm round cake pan and dust with flour; shake the pan to remove any excess flour.

In a large mixing bowl, beat the butter and the sugar until creamy. Add the eggs and juice and continue to beat. In a small mixing bowl, mix the flour and baking powder. Sift over the butter mixture and blend until smooth.

Pour the batter into the prepared pan. Bake until a toothpick poked into the cake comes out clean, 25 to 35 minutes. Let cool.

MEANWHILE, PREPARE THE GLAZE. In a small saucepan, whisk the juice and sugar. Cut the clementine in half crosswise and then cut each half into four or six slices. Add the slices to the pan. Cook uncovered over medium heat, stirring from time to time, until the liquid is reduced to a syrupy glaze, about 25 minutes. Let cool to room temperature or just slightly warm.

To serve, slice the cake into thick wedges. Place a piece or two of candied clementine on top of each wedge and drizzle with the glaze.

Sweet couscous makes for an attractive and filling dessert or snack. The mounds of couscous are decoratively patterned with raisins, almonds, and, if desired, dates. Traditionally, the couscous is served with glasses of cold milk. For a refreshing touch, add a few drops of orange flower water to the milk.

SWEET COUSCOUS

seffa

SERVES 4

About 1⅓ cups/225 g fine-grain couscous

¼ cup/55 g butter, softened

About ½ cup/60 g powdered sugar, plus more for dusting

⅛ tsp orange flower water, plus for more adding to the milk

Scant ½ cup/60 small golden raisins

Ground cinnamon for dusting

½ cup/60 g unsalted toasted almonds without skins

8 to 12 large dates, such as *mejhoul*, pitted and halved lengthwise (optional)

4 cups/1 L cold milk

Prepare the couscous following the directions on page 171, omitting the oil. Transfer the warm grains to a large, wide mixing bowl or *gsâa*. Using your hands, work the butter, powdered sugar, and ⅛ tsp orange flower water into the couscous. Blend in the raisins.

On a large serving platter or dish, gently mound the couscous into a dome shape without pressing or packing it down. Make decorative lines with cinnamon and powdered sugar. Place the almonds and the dates (if desired) around the couscous in an attractive pattern.

Serve with individual bowls of milk to spoon over the couscous. If desired, add a few drops of orange flower water to each serving of milk.

DRINKS

Spiced Coffee
qehwa m'attar
• 209 •

Mint Tea
atay bil naânaâ
• 210 •

Saffron Tea
• 211 •

Milky Tea with Oregano,
Aniseed, and Lavender
kandra
• 212 •

Almond Milk with
Orange Flower Water
• 213 •

Chilled Cucumber and Orange Juice
with Oregano
• 214 •

The king of the Moroccan beverages is, undeniably, Mint Tea (page 210). Brewed in teapots and served in small, often ornate glasses, tea is invariably sweet—just sweet enough to make you a little thirsty. In winter, when mint tends to be at its weakest, many add to the pot other fresh herbs, such as absinthe, marjoram, or verbena. Customarily brewed in and served from a silver teapot called *berrad* (see page 55), the tea is poured into short, often ornate tea glasses from well above the glass. A scientific explanation might be that this practice reoxygenates the water, which was flattened in the process of boiling. But as one Fassi told me, the sound of hot, cascading tea is a way of saying, "Pay attention to your host!"

Among other hot drinks are many herbal infusions, with lemon verbena being widely popular for its lovely flavor and also its calming and digestive benefits. I have had tisanes of thyme, of oregano, and of sage, and numerous blends, from fresh absinthe with dried rosebuds in the northern coastal town of Asilah to lavender, mint, and rosemary in the western slopes of the High Atlas. Herbs such as thyme and oregano are infused into warm milk, and cold milk and almond milk (see page 212) can be perfumed with a few drops of orange flower water or rose water. The ancient tradition of Spiced Coffee (facing page) might be less popular today, yet is still enjoyed by many.

Stalls that offer freshly squeezed juices are numerous in cities. In homes, orange juice is the base for many fruit drinks and is blended with a wide array of ingredients, from watermelon to cucumber (see page 214). Avocado puréed into juices thickens them, making them both refreshing and filling.

Although spiced coffee isn't as popular in Morocco as it once was—having been eclipsed by espresso—it's still enjoyed around the country by coffee aficionados. I have found *café épicé* in homes (where the heady smell of the brewing coffee is dazzling), in places in the countryside, and in certain medina cafés, the kind where older men gather to play cards and talk politics.

Cinnamon, ginger, clove, aniseed, nutmeg, freshly ground black or white pepper—these are some of the classic spices that give the drink its name. Friends in Morocco, self-confessed coffee aficionados, add toasted sesame seeds to their brews for a slightly nutty, savory flavor. One grinds four toasted chickpeas with the coffee beans and spices.

The measurements here are general. Much depends on the roast and grind of the coffee, and the desired strength of both the brew and the level of spice. Ideally, grind the coffee beans and spices together just before preparing.

The directions below are for preparing the coffee in a saucepan, which allows the recipe to easily be doubled or tripled. To prepare in a stove-top espresso maker—one of the popular pots with two parts that screw together, such as the Bialetti Moka Express—mix the spices and coffee and prepare as usual for a two- or three-serving pot.

SPICED COFFEE

qehwa m'attar

SERVES 2

Heaped 2 Tbsp ground coffee

⅛ tsp ground cinnamon

2 pinches aniseed

2 pinches ground ginger

2 pinches freshly ground white or black pepper

1 pinch freshly grated nutmeg

2 cardamom pods, crushed

1 tsp toasted sesame seeds

Sugar

In a small bowl, mix together the coffee, spices, and sesame seeds.

In a saucepan, bring 2 cups/480 ml water to a boil. Add the coffee mixture, stir well, and let boil and foam for 1 minute, watching that it does not boil over. Remove from the heat, stir again, and cover. Let sit undisturbed for 4 to 5 minutes.

Gently pour the coffee into cups through a fine-mesh strainer to catch the finer grounds, herbs, and seeds. Sweeten with sugar as desired and serve.

Steeped with fresh spearmint leaves and sweetened with plenty of sugar, mint tea is drunk by every class of person throughout the day—as an apéritif, as a digestive, and as an accompaniment to meals, with grilled foods and with sweets.

Ways of preparing differ from house to house, as do strengths of the tea. In Fès and Meknès, for instance, a more delicate, golden tone is often preferred, whereas in the south, the tea tends to be stronger and darker. In winter, sprigs of fresh absinthe leaves (*shiba*, see page 47) are commonly added to the pot. Especially in Marrakech and the Atlas, other fresh herbs, such as marjoram, sage, and verbena, are paired with the mint.

Moroccans use loose-leaf Chinese gunpowder green tea leaves. Rinsing the leaves in the pot with boiling water removes some of the bitterness and allows the tea to steep longer with the mint. Use plenty of mint, as the brew should have almost a tingly, medicinal taste.

MINT TEA

atay bil naânaâ

SERVES 2

Level 2 tsp loose-leaf gunpowder green tea
1 cup/45 g firmly packed sprigs fresh mint or
    a blend of mint and other fresh herbs, plus
    sprigs for garnishing
2 Tbsp sugar, plus more if needed

In a kettle or saucepan, bring 3¼ cups/770 ml water to a rolling boil. Keep at a boil while preparing the tea.

In a teapot, place the tea leaves. Pour ½ cup/ 120 ml of the boiling water over the leaves. Let the teapot sit undisturbed for 10 seconds and then swirl it for 5 seconds. Pour out all the water, using a strainer if needed to ensure that none of the tea leaves escapes.

Pour another ½ cup/120 ml of the boiling water into the teapot, immediately swirl, and pour out all of the water, again making sure none of the tea leaves escapes.

Fill the teapot with the remaining 2¼ cups/ 530 ml boiling water. Place the mint in the teapot and press down with a spoon to gently crush it. Sprinkle in the sugar. Cover and let steep undisturbed for 2 minutes. Pour a glass of tea and return it to the pot. Repeat two or three more times to dissolve the sugar and blend the flavors. Taste for sweetness, adding more sugar if necessary or steeping the tea a bit longer to make it stronger.

Pour into clear tea glasses through a strainer, garnish with mint sprigs, and serve.

Although fresh mint usually flavors pots of green tea, other herbs are used, such as a local oregano called *zaâtar* in the oasis of Erfoud and saffron in one Anti-Atlas town. Saffron is an important crop around Taliouine on the high Souktana plateau, where the fragrant flower stigmas season many dishes and also lace tea.

Rinsing the leaves in the pot with boiling water first removes some of the bitterness and darkness, and allows the saffron's flavor and golden hues to come through.

SAFFRON TEA

SERVES 2

½ Tbsp loose-leaf gunpowder green tea
24 to 30 saffron threads
1½ Tbsp sugar, plus more, if needed
4 sprigs fresh mint for garnishing

In a kettle or saucepan, bring 2½ cups/600 ml water to a rolling boil. Keep at a boil while preparing the tea.

In a teapot, place the tea leaves. Pour ½ cup/120 ml of the boiling water over the leaves. Let the teapot sit undisturbed for 10 seconds and then swirl it for 5 seconds. Pour out all the water, using a strainer if needed to ensure that none of the tea leaves escapes.

Add the saffron and sugar to the pot. Pour the remaining 2 cups/480 ml boiling water into the teapot, cover, and infuse for 4 minutes. Pour a glass of tea and return it to the pot. Repeat two or three more times to dissolve the sugar and blend the flavors. Taste for sweetness, adding more sugar if necessary or steeping the tea a bit longer to make stronger.

Pour into clear tea glasses through a strainer, garnish with mint sprigs, and serve.

This milky Moroccan chai called *kandra* comes from around Sidi Ifni, an isolated fishing town in the southern Anti-Atlas mountains. The complexly flavored drink is made with gunpowder green tea and savory oregano, lavender, and aniseed for their heady aromas. A tear of reddish brown gum arabic gives the tea a silky viscosity. I was introduced to the special tea by Malika Essaidi while hanging around Sidi Ifni one winter, and it remains for me a perfect winter brew.

MILKY TEA WITH OREGANO, ANISEED, AND LAVENDER

kandra

SERVES 2

Heaped 3 tsp loose-leaf gunpowder green tea
Generous 1 Tbsp dried oregano or *zaâtar*
  (see page 48)
½ tsp dried lavender
½ tsp aniseed
1½ cups/360 ml milk
1½ Tbsp sugar, plus more if needed
1 tear gum arabic (see page 50)

In a small flameproof teapot or saucepan, place the tea leaves.

In a kettle or saucepan, bring ½ cup/120 ml water to a boil. Pour the boiling water over the tea leaves. Swirl the teapot for 5 seconds and pour out all the water, using a strainer if needed to ensure that none of the tea leaves escapes.

Add the oregano, lavender, and aniseed to the teapot and pour in the milk. Bring to a gentle boil over medium heat, about 6 minutes, watching that it does not boil over. Remove from the heat and add the sugar and gum arabic. Pour a glass of tea and return it to the pot. Repeat two or three times to dissolve the sugar and blend the flavors. Taste for sweetness, adding more sugar if necessary or steeping the tea a bit longer to make stronger.

Pour into glasses through a strainer and serve.

This refreshing, festive drink is popular in homes and also to sip while lingering with friends on café terraces. The almond flavor is delicate, so be careful when adding the orange flower water.

ALMOND MILK WITH ORANGE FLOWER WATER

SERVES 4

½ cup/60 g ground almonds
6 Tbsp/75 g superfine sugar
3 cups/720 ml milk
16 drops or so orange flower water

In a small saucepan, heat 1 cup/240 ml water until hot. In a mixing bowl, put the almonds and sugar and cover with the hot water. Stir and let sit for 5 minutes. Add the milk and let sit for another 5 minutes, stirring from time to time.

Strain through a very fine sieve, a tea strainer, or cheesecloth into a pitcher. Press or squeeze all the liquid from the almonds; discard the solids. Refrigerate until well chilled.

Add the orange flower water, stir, and divide among tall glasses. Serve very cold.

Moroccans love fresh juices, and the combinations they make are eclectic and highly seasonal. This is one of my favorites. Although it is commonly prepared as a juice, it can also be a drinkable dessert, especially on warm summer days. I once had it as a "salad" served with a spoon—like Grated Carrot and Orange Salad (page 102)—in late fall in the eastern High Atlas. Oranges hadn't yet ripened, and instead the cook used small clementines from down the valley. Served before a communal platter of Berber Barley Couscous with Vegetables (page 174), the drink seemed closer to a light, sophisticated, vibrant green gazpacho than a rustic salad.

CHILLED CUCUMBER AND ORANGE JUICE WITH OREGANO

SERVES 6

2 lb/910 g medium cucumbers

2¼ cups/530 ml fresh orange or mandarin orange juice, preferably clementine

1½ tsp superfine sugar, plus more as needed

½ tsp dried oregano or *zaâtar* (see page 48), plus more as needed

Trim the ends from the cucumbers and scrub the peels. Remove about half of the peels from each cucumber and remove the seeds if they are large. Cut the cucumber into chunks and put in a food processor or blender. Pour in the orange juice and sprinkle in the sugar and oregano. Blend for at least 1 minute or until very finely puréed. The drink should be a bit thick and slightly foamy. Taste for sweetness and seasoning and adjust as needed.

Pour into a pitcher, cover, and refrigerate until chilled. Serve in tall glasses or in small bowls with spoons.

SELECTED BIBLIOGRAPHY

Agourram, Touria. *De mère en fille: La cuisine marocaine*. Paris: Albin Michel, 2000.

Alami, Fouziya, and Souâd El Mansouri. *Cuisine pour Ramadan et fêtes*. Casablanca: Najah El Jadida, 1996.

Amhaouche, Rachida. *Pâtisserie marocaine*. Casablanca: Chaaraoui, 2005.

Andalusian Morocco: A Discovery in Living Art. Rabat: Museum With No Frontiers, 2002.

Bellahsen, Fabien, and Daniel Rouche. *Délices du Maroc*. Paris: Editions de Lodi, 2005.

Benayoun, Aline. *Casablanca Cuisine: French North African Cooking*. London: Serif, 1998.

Benkirane, Fettouma. *Délices de Ramadan*. Mohammedia, Morocco: Librairie Nationale, 2006.

Bennani-Smirès, Latifa. *La cuisine marocaine*. Casablanca: Al Madariss, 2004.

Charkor, Salah. *Traité de gastronomie marocaine*. Tanger: Le Journal de Tanger, 2008.

Choumicha. *Choumicha Ch'hiwate: cuisine marocaine*. Casablanca: Librairie Al Ouma, 2005.

Danan, Simy, and Jacques Denarnaud. *La nouvelle cuisine judéo-marocaine*. Paris: ACR Edition, 1994.

Fedel, Mohamed. *Saveurs du Maroc*. Paris: Editions de Lodi, 2006.

Goldstein, Joyce. *Saffron Shores*. San Francisco: Chronicle Books, 2002.

Guinaudeau, Madame. *Traditional Moroccan Cooking: Recipes from Fez*. Translated by J. E. Harris. London: Serif, 2003.

Hal, Fatema. *The Food of Morocco*. Singapore: Periplus, 2002.

Harrak, Hasnaâ, and Abdelaziz Chetto. *Valorisation et commercialisation des dattes au Maroc*. Marrakech: INRA, 2001.

Hemphill, Ian. *Spice Notes: A Cook's Compendium of Herbs and Spices*. Sydney: Macmillan, 2000.

Koehler, Jeff. *Rice Pasta Couscous: The Heart of the Mediterranean Kitchen*. San Francisco: Chronicle Books, 2009.

Mallos, Tess. *A Little Taste of Morocco*. Sydney: Murdoch, 2006.

Morse, Kitty. *Cooking at the Kasbah*. San Francisco: Chronicle Books, 1998.

Morsy, Magali. *Recetas a base de couscous*. Barcelona: Parsifal, 1999.

Norman, Jill. *Herbs & Spices: The Cook's Reference*. New York: DK, 2002.

Pennell, C. R. *Morocco: From Empire to Independence*. Oxford: Oneworld, 2003.

Roden, Claudia. *The New Book of Middle Eastern Food*. New York: Alfred A. Knopf, 2000.

Rogerson, Barnaby. *A Traveller's History of North Africa*. Gloucestershire, UK: Windrush, 1998.

Rough Guide to Morocco. 9th ed. London: Rough Guides, 2010.

Sijelmassi, Abdelhaï. *Les plantes médicinales du Maroc*. Casablanca: Editions La Fennec, 2008.

Wolfert, Paula. *Couscous and Other Good Food from Morocco*. New York: Harper & Row, 1973.

Wright, Clifford A. *A Mediterranean Feast*. New York: William Morrow, 1999.

ACKNOWLEDGMENTS

I would first like to thank the generous hospitality I found across Morocco, and the countless shop owners, butchers, waiters, chefs called from the kitchen, fishermen, farmers, shepherds, and fellow shoppers and diners who patiently answered my questions. A special thanks to those who generously allowed me into their kitchen to show me *their* Moroccan cuisine. *Shukran!*

The book owes a debt to Chakib Ghadouani at the Moroccan National Tourist Office, who has been a source of ideas and information from the start, and shared everything he could about Morocco—including his mother's cooking. And thank you to José Abete and Fabrizio Ruspoli, who have been welcoming, good company, and very helpful on my many times through Marrakech. And to Mohammed Nahir for so freely sharing his breadth of Moroccan culinary knowledge.

The following stand out in Morocco for their assistance:

IN THE NORTH: Philippe Guiguet-Bologne and Abdellatif Ouafik at Dar Nour (Tanger); Louis Soubrier and Zohra Kanfoud (Tanger); Khadija Oualili, Anne-Judith Van Loock, and Ahmed Benrradiya (Asilah); Ruth Barreto Ramos at El Reducto (Tétouan); Jaber El Hababi at Auberge Dardara (Rif); and mushroom guides Mohammed Elafia and son Nafia (Rif).

IN FÈS AND THE MIDDLE ATLAS: Jawhar Yassir, Abdelkader Bensdira, and Mounia Mousaid at Riad El Amine (Fès); Cherghi Nefisse (Fès); Adnane Snoussi (Fès); and Chef Mohamed Oumadan at Hôtel Panorama (Azrou).

ON THE ATLANTIC COAST: Meriem Kherchouf, Ahmed Ghadouani, and Siham Hatta (Rabat); Fadel Mounir (Rabat); Moncif Rahali at Le Ziryab (Rabat); Saïd Mouhid (Casablanca); Rachid and Chantal El Ouariti and Mina Selouani at Riad Le Mazagao (El Jadida); Jean-Michel and Hanane Gendrot at Riad Safi (Safi); Karim Beniounes (Safi); Khadija Benchaalal and Christine Renault at Villa Garnace (Essaouira); and Abdellah Messate (Essaouira).

IN MARRAKECH AND THE HIGH ATLAS: José Abete, Fabrizio Ruspoli, Rachid Edhidi, and *dadas* LaAziza and Fatiha at La Maison Arabe; Andrea and Bernd Kolb, Housna Hajby, and Khadija Dilali at AnaYela; Meryanne Loum-Martin, Bahija Lafridi, and Erin Smith at Jnane Tamsna; attar Abderrahim Kalaaji; and Mohammed Nahir (Marrakech); Ahmed Agouni, Catherine Rophé, and the cooks at Irocha (Tisseldeï); Jean-Martin Herbeq, Olivier Deschamps, Thierry Tarot, Habiba Irich, Wafa Saadi, and Latifa Boulaqtib at Terres d'Amanar (Ourika).

IN CENTRAL MOROCCO AND THE ANTI-ATLAS: Aïcha Boutkhoum at Dar Daïf (Ouarzazate); Aziz Machkour at Dar Mouna (Aït Benhaddou); Abderahim Ougarane (Timiderte); the women at Coopérative Féminine Tamounte (Imin'tlit); and Antoine Bouillon and Raja Salhi at Dar Raha (Zagora).

THE SAHARA AND THE DEEP SOUTH: Pierre Gerbens and Ali Amrou at Fort Bou-Jerif (Guelmim); Michèle Ménuel-Pinat, Yann Pinat, and Zoubida Azouzi at Bab el Maâder (Tiznit); the women at Coopérative Féminine d'Argane Tafyoucht (Mesti); Malika Essaidi at La Suerte Loca (Sidi Ifni); Paul Italiano and family at La Courbine d'Argent (Sidi Akhfennir, Laâyoune); and Mostafa Aliane.

I am grateful to Tod Nelson, Jim Finley, Kirk Giloth, Robert Brown, and Caspar for their continued insight into writing, and to Mark Gregory Peters and Kevin Miyazaki for theirs into photography. Also to Jodi Liano, Tori Ritchie, and Leslie Jonath in San Francisco; Rebecca Staffel in Seattle; Heather Hartley, Jeffrey Greene, Eddy Harris, John Baxter, and Sylvia Whitman in Paris; and Virginia Irurita in Madrid.

In Barcelona, special thanks to Sanae Nouali and Sandra Martínez, my in-laws Tomàs and Rosa, my sisters-in-law (Carmina, Rosa María, and Marien) and their husbands (Robert, Rámon, and Xicu, respectively), Cesc Segura and Eli Jaso, Cristina Chiva and Dani Cárdenas, and Eugenia Sarasqueta.

I thank my family in the United States, especially my parents Bill and Joanne, who supported this book in many ways, as well as my grandparents, aunts and uncles, cousins, and brother Bill and his wife, Sarah.

And warm thanks to Naomi Duguid, who continues to generously offer a stream of ideas, advice, and creative support that goes beyond the culinary.

Also thanks to the various editors and food professionals who have supported my cooking, writing, and photographing over the years, including Dana Bowen, Paul Love, and James Oseland at *Saveur*; Jocelyn Zuckerman at *Gourmet*; Kate Heddings and Tina Ujlaki at *Food & Wine*; Derk Richardson and April Kilcrease at *Afar*; Justin Paul and Marika Cain at *Virtuoso Life*; Jeanne McManus at the *Washington Post*; Catharine Hamm and Craig Nakano at the *Los Angeles Times*; Jennifer Wolcott at the *Christian Science Monitor*; Allison Cleary and Patsy Jamieson at *EatingWell*; Dick Doughty and Sarah Miller at *Saudi Aramco World*; and Michelle Wildgen at *Tin House*. Also, Katie Workman and Mary Goodbody at Cookstr.com, Sandy Gluck and Lisa Mantineo at Martha Stewart Living Radio, and Mary Risley at Tante Marie's Cooking School in San Francisco.

As always, deep-felt appreciation to my superb agent Doe Coover (and those in her office, including Frances Kennedy) for offering feedback, opinions, and help with the initial idea.

At Chronicle Books I thank my editors Bill LeBlond and Amy Treadwell, assistant editor Sarah Billingsley; Peter Perez and David Hawk in marketing; Alice Chau for her extraordinary design; Ann Spradlin, Doug Ogan, and Claire Fletcher on the managing editorial team; and Lorena Jones. Thanks also to Judith Dunham for her eagle-eyed copyediting and Joseph Ternes for his past work on my Web site, www.jeff-koehler.com.

And finally to Eva, Alba, and Maia—wonderful, patient companions on the road, faithful helpers in the kitchen (measuring, adding, stirring), and, most important, tasters, eating Moroccan cuisine almost daily, and giving their opinions on every recipe in this book more than once.

INDEX